Media Organizations and Convergence

Case Studies of Media Convergence Pioneers

LEA'S COMMUNICATION SERIES

Jennings Bryant / Dolf Zillmann, General Editors

Selected titles in Mass Communication
(Alan Rubin, Advisory Editor) include:

Albarran/Arrese • Time and Media Markets

Alexander/Owers/Carveth/Hollifield/Greco • Media Economics: Theory and Practice, Third Edition

Compaine/Gomery • Who Owns the Media? Competition and Concentration in the Mass Media Industry, Third Edition

Harris • A Cognitive Psychology of Mass Communication, Third Edition

Moore • Mass Communication Law and Ethics, Second Edition

Perse • Media Effects and Society

Price • The V-Chip Debate: Content Filtering From Television to the Internet

For a complete list of titles in LEA's Communication Series, please contact Lawrence Erlbaum Associates, Publishers at www.erlbaum.com

Media Organizations and Convergence

Case Studies of Media Convergence Pioneers

Gracie Lawson-Borders, PhD
Kent State University

LAWRENCE ERLBAUM ASSOCIATES, PUBLISHERS

2006   Mahwah, New Jersey   London

Lawrence Erlbaum Associates, Inc., Publishers
10 Industrial Avenue
Mahwah, New Jersey 07430
www.erlbaum.com

Cover design by Kathryn Houghtaling Lacey

Library of Congress Cataloging-in-Publication Data

Lawson-Borders, Gracie.
Media organizations and convergence : case studies of media
convergence pioneers / by Gracie Lawson-Borders.
p.   cm. — (LEA's communication series)
Includes bibliographical references and index.
ISBN 0-8058-5031-7 (cloth : alk. paper)
ISBN 0-8058-5032-5 (pbk. : alk. paper)
1. Mass media—Technological innovations—United States.
I. Title.   II. Series.
P96.T422U6357   2005
302.23—dc22
2005049488
CIP

Books published by Lawrence Erlbaum Associates are
printed on acid-free paper, and their bindings are chosen for
strength and durability.

Printed in the United States of America
10   9   8   7   6   5   4   3   2   1

To my husband Floyd and mother Bettye
for their love, support, and encouragement.

Contents

Preface   ix

Acknowledgments   xiii

I MEDIA ORGANIZATIONS AND CONVERGENCE

1 Introduction: The Many Faces of Convergence   3

2 Traditional Media and Business Practices   27

3 Theoretical Implications   43

II CONVERGENCE IN ACTION

4 Tribune Company: A Convergence Pioneer   69
      Since the 1900s

5 Media General: A Temple to Convergence—   97
      The News Center in Tampa, Florida

6 Belo Corporation: Market Dominance in Dallas   127

CONCLUSION

7   Social Capital: Implications for Convergence   161

8   The Future of Convergence   183

      Author Index   201

      Subject Index   205

Preface

This book is about the story of media convergence, or rather a snapshot at this moment and time into its evolving history in the media industry. Media convergence has been defined in many ways, but its most simplistic definition is the combining of old (traditional) media with new media for the dissemination of news, information, and entertainment. This could occur as content or product. Technological advancements, combined with computer-driven delivery of content, have accelerated the information age. Today, emerging digital technologies have created the ability to reach beyond even the dreams realized by early American inventor Samuel Morse and the cryptic Morse code he developed for the telegraph that was viewed as revolutionary communication in the 19th century. Tom Standage (1998) called this early cryptic communication process a forbearer of technology to come in his book, *The Victorian Internet: The Remarkable Story of the Telegraph and the Nineteenth Century's On-line Pioneers.* Today the Internet captures the awe and imagination of users and developers of content for use across the electronic medium. The Internet is joined by a plethora of communication channels that cross multiple boundaries and platforms and continue to expand in new directions from the personal PC to PDAs, digital cell phones, digital video recorders, satellites, and more. Nowhere in the history of the development of machinery and technology has it become more apparent that new inventions and ideas have transformed the telecommunications and media industries into realms that are only limited by the imagination of modern-day inventors.

This book is an exploration of technology's impact on media companies and journalistic, business, and economic practices that have been adjusted to meet the changes. The book is comprised of two parts. Part I is entitled *Media Organizations and Convergence.* Chapter 1 examines the many definitions of *convergence* and explores the changes in communication technologies. The chapter examines the challenges the new media environment creates for media companies as they try to meet the changing needs of their audiences, or an interchangeable set of terms that include *users, viewers*, and *readers* depending on the platform accessed. This chapter examines how digital technology has opened the door for convergence with faster and more diverse delivery channels. Seven Observations of Convergence are introduced that serve as best practices for the convergence process to be operationalized within media organizations. Several models of convergence practices are examined to situate the discussion of the strategies and tactics of media organizations to digital delivery of content.

Chapter 2 is a brief history of different mediums and their evolution as they adapt to emerging technologies, media conglomeration, and the competitive and global changes that have occurred in the industry. MIT's Henry Jenkins (2001) argued that "one box" will not deliver all of the content produced by media (p. 93). The cultural, global, economic, technological, and social implications of convergence are too far reaching to aggregate media content into one delivery system. Most people view their PCs and TVs as different mediums used primarily for information retrieval and entertainment, respectively. Media and electronic manufacturers are grabbling to determine whether the public will change such habits.

Chapter 3 examines the theoretical implications of technology and convergence in the operations and practices of media organizations. Everett Rogers' diffusion of innovations is used to examine the five stages of the innovation process within organizations. The diffusion of innovations is integrated with innovation management research to assess the impact of emerging technologies for media organizations. Research into new media technologies must also address the concerns of audience. Therefore, research on the uses and gratifications theoretical approach is used to illustrate the audience perspective on use of technologies for delivery of content. The adage from the movie *Field of Dreams*, "If you build it, they will come," is assessed in the digital environment to argue that just building it (some technology, whether hardware or software) does not necessarily mean audiences will come. Uses and gratifications research provides a perspective to examine the needs and motivations of users.

Part II, *Convergence in Action,* includes case studies of media convergence pioneers, three large media conglomerates that incorporate convergence as part of their journalistic practices and how they conduct business. The media companies are Tribune Company in Chicago, Media-General of Richmond, Virginia, and Belo Corporation in Dallas. Chapters 4, 5, and 6 are case studies devoted to each company that tell a story about the development of the convergence process in markets where the company owns the print, broadcast, and online outlets, and the goal is to converge content daily. Research at these organizations occurred over the past 3 years, beginning in the summer of 2002, using in-depth interviews, internal and external documents, and participant observations of the daily work process. The business properties studied for each media company include Tribune's operations in Chicago, Belo's in Dallas, and Media General's in Tampa at The News Center.

Finally, chapter 7 examines the social, cultural, and political implications of convergence. Media effects are enhanced because of the reach and depth of media content as a result of emerging technologies. In June 2003, the Federal Communications Commission (FCC) relaxed the rules on cross-ownership of media in different markets. In 2004, a federal appeals court stayed the change. However, the implications of a change in the cross-ownership ban are far reaching and could facilitate a new wave of mergers, acquisitions, and media consolidation.

Chapter 8 addresses the future of convergence with a snapshot of the concept and process at this point and time in history. I identify seven issues that serve as signposts to watch for changes in production, distribution, and dissemination of content through new technologies. The visceral nature of the media industry makes it evident that this concluding chapter is just the beginning of the ongoing conversation about convergence.

REFERENCES

Jenkins, H. (2001). Convergence? I diverge. *Technology Review, 104*(5), 93.

Standage, T. (1998). *Victorian internet: The remarkable story of the telegraph and the nineteenth century's on-line pioneers.* New York: Walker & Company.

Acknowledgments

A project such as this could not be completed without the support of numerous people, and I am eternally grateful for their assistance. The project has been supported in part by research funds provided by Kent State University and a grant from Southern Methodist University's University Research Council. There are too many people to name individually, but there are some people I would like to specifically thank, including Dr. Alan Rubin for his guidance and support to get this book off the ground, and my book editor, Linda Bathgate. Several people helped to facilitate my field research at the various media companies, which enabled this project to get started. They are Chris Kelley, editor, *Belo Interactive Dallas*; Pat Mitchell, senior presentation editor, *The Tampa Tribune at The News Center*; and Ann Marie Lipinski, vice president and executive editor, *The Chicago Tribune*. Thanks to the numerous other people whom I interviewed and assisted me while in the field at the three media locations. A special thanks to my copyeditor, Karen Burroughs Hannsberry, for her work on the early manuscript. Last, but not least, I would like to thank my husband Floyd for his love and support for all of my endeavors.

—Gracie Lawson-Borders
Kent State University
January 2005

I

Media Organizations and Convergence

1

Introduction: The Many Faces of Convergence[1]

What is convergence? *Convergence* is an elusive term that is used in multiple contexts and is often ambiguous in its definition. The definitions discussed next provide insight into the variations for understanding convergence. According to the Missouri Group (cited in Brooks, Kennedy, Moen, & Ranly, 2004), convergence from a journalism perspective is "the practice of sharing and cross-promoting content from a variety of media, some interactive, through newsroom collaborations and partnerships" (p. 15). A definition by Wirtz (1999) focuses on multimedia applications, stating:

Convergence can be defined as the dynamic approach or partial integration of different communication and information-based market applications. A further aspect of convergence is that it brings out integrated multimedia products and services that render possible the satisfaction of additional and multiple consumer preferences. (p. 15)

Seib (2001) suggested, "Convergence involves marrying the slick format of television to the almost infinite information-providing capacity of the Internet" (p. 7). A. Nachison of the American Press Institute's Media Center defined *convergence* as "the strategic, operational, product and cultural union of print, audio, video and

---

[1]An earlier version of this chapter appeared as G. Lawson-Borders (2003). Integrating new media and old media: Seven observations of convergence as a strategy for best practices in media organizations, *The International Journal on Media Management*, 5(2), 91–99. Reprinted by permission.

interactive digital information services and organizations" (A. Nachison, personal communication, August 2002).

Northwestern University new media scholar Gordon (2003) provided a historical look at the term *convergence* that dates back to the *Oxford English Dictionary* in the 17th and 18th centuries, when English scientist William Derham used the term to describe his experiments measuring the speed of sound. Gordon suggested convergence has been used to describe everything from "wind currents, mathematical series, nonparallel lines, and evolutionary biology" (p. 58).

The meaning of convergence evolved by the 1960s and 1970s when the U.S. Department of Defense (DOD) began work with researchers and universities to develop the networked system now known as the Internet. The storage of data digitally increased the possibilities of integrating information. Discussions of convergence of technologies and industries have been integrated into the popular vernacular beginning with de Sola Pool's (1983), *Technologies of Freedom*, continuing with Negroponte's (1995) *Being Digital* on moving from atoms to a series of 0s and 1s to transmit data, and concluding in the 1990s when convergence hit the popular press. The concept of convergence catapulted into our conscience in 2000 when the highly publicized AOL and Time Warner $166 billion stock merger was announced as the unheralded convergence of a new (Internet) and old (cable) media company (Gordon, 2003). The rise and ultimate failure of that merger resulted in AOL being dropped from the stock ticker and company name in 2003. An extensive and comprehensive review of convergence definitions could go on for several chapters. However, most of the definitions include the blending of technological capabilities to deliver content.

For purposes of this book, I define *convergence as the realm of possibilities when cooperation occurs between print and broadcast for the delivery of multimedia content through the use of computers and the Internet.* This definition is based on a model (Fig. 1.1) in which convergence is driven by the intersection of content through numerous platforms by using computers and the Internet. The content that gets there, and the manner in which it

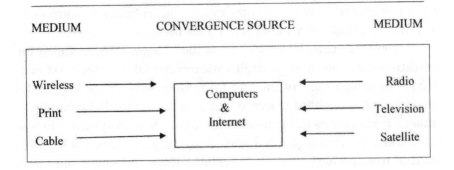

FIG. 1.1. Convergence definition model.

arrives, in that combination of text, audio, and video, is central to the decision.

Today, media organizations reflect this realm of possibilities by maximizing the use of the content they produce on several platforms. Dallas-based Belo's C. Kelley stated his company's goal in electronic delivery is to provide the "immediacy of television, the urgency of the Internet, and the depth of newspapers" (personal communication, June 3, 2002). Few media organizations would argue against this objective in a multimedia environment as they strive to meet users and audiences in numerous ways. Media companies recognize the changing demographics and needs of their audiences and work to use their various business units to optimize content delivery. The question that most media executives must ask is not whether their organization is a newspaper, TV station, radio, movie, or cable company. The more pertinent questions might be: "Are we in the content business? What are the complementary channels to deliver that content?"

A survey by the Pew Center for Civic Journalism in 2000 found that 9 out of 10 editors from 360 newspapers stated that more interactivity with readers was key to the future of their business (cited in Schaffer, 2001). The interactivity provided with online content delivered through the computer is enticing for traditional and new media organizations. The old one-way model of mass communication from one source to many must adjust in the converged world to a two-way communication from many sources to reach individuals in an interactive new media environment.

Convergence can also be viewed as the window of opportunity for traditional media to align itself with technologies of the 21st century. The digitization of media and information technology is the major impetus behind convergence (Gershon, 2000). Digital technology compresses information and allows text, graphics, photos, and audio to be transmitted across media platforms. As we have moved from an agricultural, to an industrial, and now to an information-driven society, technology has been a central catalyst. The phenomenal growth of the Internet from the introduction of the Mosaic graphical browser to PDF files, audio and streaming video has resulted in a rapid expansion of online content for assessing information electronically. Changing demographics and competing messages made the Internet particularly attractive to traditional print and broadcast media that sought to protect their brand and their historical specialty of gathering and disseminating news, information, and entertainment.

According to Nielsen Media Research, 57 million copies of newspapers were sold daily in 2000, and 25 to 30 million people watched TV network newscasts (cited in Barringer, 2001). By September 2001, approximately 143 million Americans were using the Internet, which is about 54% of the population (U.S. Department of Commerce, 2002). The Internet has become a viable source of news and information. The integration of content across platforms to connect these audiences (e.g., people who access or use the Internet and computers) is part of the goal of convergence in media organizations.

This book focuses on convergence as both a concept and a process by examining several questions that are raised in discussions of convergence. The first half of the book examines numerous questions applicable to convergence. What are the various definitions of convergence? What does convergence mean to content providers? Data can be accessed through the Internet, computers, or traditional print and broadcast platforms; what do we call people who access content through the Internet? Do we call them users, audiences, viewers, readers, or customers? What theoretical issues help explain the use and adoption of emerging communication technologies by both content providers and users? Are the various media platforms being used in ways envisioned by their creators? What are the strategies used by leading media organizations to develop content and create and maintain both an online and an offline presence?

The second half of the book includes case studies of convergence in action at three large U.S. media organizations that are considered convergence pioneers because of their top–down organizational commitment to convergence practices. The case studies focus on Tribune Company's Chicago media operations, Belo Corporation's Dallas properties, and Media General's The News Center in Tampa, Florida. In each market, the parent company owns at least one major newspaper, TV station, Web site, and, in some markets, radio station, cable outlet, or cable superstation in which content can be converged daily across platforms.

The Dean of the School of Journalism at the University of Kansas, James Gentry, stated there were some 50 media partnerships or affiliations across the United States practicing convergence in 2001. Gentry suggested that this is due to "increased advertising revenue brought about by higher ratings, more subscribers, or more website traffic" (cited in Wendland, 2001, par. 11). The American Press Institute (API) on its Web site americanpressinstitute.com hosts an interactive feature entitled *Convergence Tracker*. The API site asks users to voluntarily submit examples of convergence mergers, partnerships, and alliances across the country. By January 2004, a graphic showing a map of the United States had 28 states color-coded as having some type of converged media operation in one or more of the markets. The Convergence Tracker identified 60 convergence relationships that include a combination of news, advertising, and outreach arrangements (Gentry, 2004). The digitization of content magnifies the speed in distribution and allows greater access by the public to media. MIT scholar and technology leader Negroponte (1995) contended in his pivotal book, *Being Digital*, that the dynamics of the digital world are far reaching:

Being digital will change the nature of mass media from a process of pushing bits at people to one of allowing people (or their computers) to pull at them. This is a radical change, because our entire concept of media is one of successive layers of filtering, which reduce information and entertainment to a collection of "top stories" or "best-sellers" to be thrown at different "audiences." (p. 84)

Negroponte taps into a salient issue; the digitization of information has transformed the relationship between media companies and their audiences. In the late 1990s, Negroponte (1995) identified three distinct and separate Vinn circles representing the Print and Publishing Industry, Broadcast and Motion Picture Industry, and Computer Industry. Negroponte predicted that by the year 2000 the three circles would overlap in a convergence of use and operations. The mergers and acquisitions activity in the media industry from the late 1990s into the 2000s are evidence of this process. Arguably, the success of such convergence has been disputed by many critics since the AOL Time Warner merger fell apart in late 2003. What remains steadfast in the industry, however, is the prolific nature of convergence, partnerships, or alliances and the reasons that so many organizations view these arrangements as key to the future of the industry and their organizations. The concerns of emerging technologies are not about one-way communication, but a two-way interactive exchange that requires content providers to offer something that the audience would select. Push-and-pull technology, where media companies push the information they want the public to have, is not sufficient in a converged environment where the audience has the power to pull only the information that best meets their needs. Media dependency theory (Ball-Rokeach, 1985) posits that an analysis of media, political, and economic systems must occur to understand media's dependency relationship to society. In this evolving world of technology and increased access to information by the public, the media and public relationship has been transformed. There is an economic and philosophical duality to convergence goals for different media organizations that are challenged by emerging technologies, with the task of finding the best ways to capture users and audiences in a dynamic multimedia environment.

Convergence is not well received because many journalists, media executives, and scholars view the process as a threat to traditional journalism values and to the practices used to gather news, information, and entertainment. However, many leading media conglomerates, electronic and PC manufacturers, and developers of hardware and software view the possibilities as unlimited for digitized content. One ardent opponent is former Poynter Institute President Robert Haiman. Haiman (2001) argued the "converged media world is one from which good journalism, and good journalists, are going to be in great need of defense" (par. 4). Despite the contentions of Haiman and others, content providers are charged with creating material laden with text, graphics, and the multimedia capabilities that are applicable to audiences in a new media environment.

These issues regarding technology and convergence are not new. In the 1960s, Canadian media scholar McLuhan (1997) acted as a "town crier," proclaiming that the media was leading us to a global society and that the "medium is the message" (p. 7). Scholars continue to debate exactly what McLuhan meant by that phrase, but whatever his intention, we have reached that global world as we sit in the infancy of the 21st century. McLuhan's predictions have been realized with the global connectedness of the Internet. Whether it is the transformation of content delivered from traditional print outlets to electronic delivery, or the digitization of data from traditional broadcast to satellite, wireless, and the Internet, the channels through which we communicate have accelerated. Fiberoptic cable has shown that the speed of light surpasses electricity, can crystallize the delivery of data, and opens up simultaneous channels. So much of this change in data and content has been facilitated by the distribution system that has pushed beyond analog to digital delivery of content. The union of technology and content delivery through computers has opened the doors to new opportunities in the media industry under convergence. Chris Kelley, editor of Belo Interactive's Dallas Web Sites, suggested that we are in a digital revolution that is powered by the convergence of different content delivery technologies.

Where convergence will lead is still unknown, but the media industry is stretching to meet the challenges journalistically and economically in an evolving multimedia environment.

NEW MEDIA

An ironic example of the influence of convergence is evident in the e-commerce world. Media scholar Campbell (2000) pointed to the fact that an irony of the success of Amazon.com is that founder Jeff Bezos used the electronic medium to sell one of the oldest mediums—books. The growth of Amazon.com, which posted its first profit in the fourth quarter of 2001, has fascinated scholars and critics who use and study the Internet. Amazon.com tapped into its audience by providing a forum that engaged users who could communicate with and shape the content they received (Kampinsky, Bowman, & Willis, 2001). Connecting one medium to another through technology and computers is an exciting change for media audiences. What is unclear for most organizations that incorporate convergence into their operations is, who is using the content they provide and why? How often do they use it? What are they willing to pay to use it? What does it take to keep users coming back to different media?

The choices for users vary from reading the newspaper in print versus accessing its online version, watching a movie preview at the theater versus linking to a movie trailer online, or watching a TV broadcast versus visiting the station's Web site in the interactive world. Interactive potential includes reading books online. An example of this dynamic experience is reading an e-book, which expands the reading process in a converged environment to an online representation of the book and a new way of interacting with the content. When Stephen King chose electronic publication for one of his novellas in 2000, the responses were as curious as the ominous nature of the topics on which he writes. More than a half a million people downloaded King's work; however, the flurry of electronic activity does not explain why the readers selected that e-book or why they would choose King or any other novelists online (Surowiecki, 2001). Western readers are taught to read from left to right. Reading on the Internet necessitates scrolling—a process that is not appealing to many readers because computer users scroll or scan when reading, which can be a daunting experience filled with the queasiness of a ferry wheel ride as your eyes and brain signals attempt to adjust to the moving computer screen. Although efforts to market e-books are improving, it seems unlikely that traditional bound and printed books are going anywhere because readers have not expressed concerns about the portability or storage capacity of books.

Since the telegraph, one medium has never completely replaced another, but rather media historians and scholars have noted that each medium builds and adapts to the one that precedes it. Radio was considered a threat to newspapers, TV was supposed to replace its predecessors, cable was predicted to unseat TV, and now satellite and the Internet loom as the latest replacement. All of these media coexist in an intricate communication delivery system that has expanded choices for the public. Yet online books are part of the growth of convergence as individuals continue to access information and entertainment across platforms. The interactivity and hypermedia use of electronic text allows moving from one screen or Web site to another, creating a dynamic experience for computer users (Fredin & David, 1998). The fascination with interactivity online will continue to draw some audiences to the experience of e-books.

The media is pervasive in society because of the ubiquitous nature of media, particularly TV and its influence since the 1950s. From the moment the alarm clock sounds in the morning and notice is taken of the manufacturer's emblem as an advertising symbol, to watching the evening news, we encounter the influence of media. Many media companies have elected to integrate the convergence process into daily operations as a tactic to address the changes in the industry. Convergence is not static, but rather a continuum in which organizations must select the appropriate medium or combination of mediums. Convergence for the sake of convergence is not advisable. Blending media forms should be the strategy when the content and the delivery programs necessitate the arrangement, according to Forrest Carr, news director of WFLA-TV in Tampa, Florida. "One of the basic truths about convergence is that not every story or tip that excites one platform is suitable for another. Sometimes a good newspaper story is just that—a good newspaper story, not suitable for TV," Carr (2002, par. 4) contended. Convergence must be sensitive to the content and the channel through which it is emitted.

Carr's TV station is a subsidiary of parent company Media General in Richmond, Virginia. Media General created a modern-day laboratory for convergence in 2000 when it opened The News Center, which houses *The Tampa Tribune*, WFLA-TV, and TBO.com. A survey in October 2001 found that the convergence operation increased *The Tampa Tribune's* exposure by 38% to the Tampa/St. Petersburg designated market area, and WFLA-TV reached 13% of the newspaper's audience (Dasbach, 2001). The media industry is taking note of the convergence experience in Tampa. At the 2002 Newspaper Association of America convention in New Orleans, some publishers disclosed incremental advertising revenue gains from convergence operations. Gannett's convergence in Phoenix with the *Arizona Republic* and NBC affiliate KPNX-TV resulted in $4 million in incremental ad revenue in 2001, but that was less than 1% of total revenues in that market (Fine, 2002). Media General collected about $6 million in incremental revenue in Tampa. However, Publisher and CEO Jim Moroney of *The Dallas Morning News* assessed these small growths in ad revenue and concluded that, although the gains were reasonable, reporting about 2% of total revenue in a given market would not impress Wall Street (Fine, 2002). As media organizations move forward, expectations for convergence from Wall Street, investors, and media executives will be for greater profits at a lesser cost.

CONVERGENCE MODELS

Convergence models vary; the most prolific has been the paid-subscription model created by the Dow Jones Company for *The Wall Street Journal* and wsj.com. The company launched its paid model in September 1996 for users to access content (Steinbock, 2000). The success of this convergence reached a milestone on December 23, 2003, when *The Wall Street Journal* ran a full-page advertisement announcing 2.6 million in paid circulation for the combined print and online *Journals*. This milestone in the organization's 114-year history prompted the start of a new advertising campaign—Total Journal—that allows advertisers to capitalize on *The Journal's* online and offline audience. *The Journal* serves a pay-subscription model that many organizations would like to emulate. The company knew its market and its brand, and it made the commitment to produce premium content for *The Journal's* electronic version equitable to its renowned print version (Steinbock, 2000). *The Journal* is the only major U.S. newspaper that has always charged a subscription fee for its Web site. The cost is $79 a year for an online subscription or $39 with a paid print subscription. The online version experienced revenues losses for several years, but the announcement in 2003 of 2.6 million paid online and offline subscriptions is noteworthy. Neil Budde, publisher of *Wall Street Journal* online, suggested the wsj.com business unit might even be profitable by the end of 2004 (cited in Gates, 2002).

The Tulsa World in eastern Oklahoma provides an example of how other media companies seek to cash in on the paid-subscription model as the industry is challenged with making online news sites profitable. In 2001, *Tulsa World* moved to a paid-subscription model for accessing its online content at TulsaWorld.com (Gates, 2002). The newspaper has about 150,000 in print circulation and 30,000 registered online subscribers. Under the pay-subscription system at *Tulsa World*, the print audience can access the Web for free, but online users (about 3,000 in 2002) paid $45 a year for access. After the first year under the paid online model, revenue from subscriptions and advertising was approximately $900,000 according to Publisher Dilene Crockett. The company experienced a 20% drop in online users when the pay model was introduced, but it eventually climbed upward. However, in Crockett's opinion, taking the plunge for paid online subscription in the long term is worth the effort (cited in Gates, 2002). Crockett suggested that, at a minimum, online newspapers need to register their users, which hundreds of newspapers started in 2002, to obtain demographic information and attract advertisers. A better understanding of the audience the media company is targeting is essential to assessing what a particular market or set of audiences is willing to bear. Both traditional media outlets and new content providers are waiting to see which model proves to be the best combination of registration, subscription, advertising, and other methods of paying for online content.

The visceral nature of the Internet becomes apparent when you examine the frequency of studies in the past couple of years conducted by government organizations, academics, market researchers, and private organizations that try to assess who is online and what they are doing while there (Online Publishers Association, 2004; Pew Internet & American Life Project, 2004; Carey, 2004; U.S. Department of Commerce, 2002). Although statistics vary from year to year and study to study, they create a picture of who is using the Internet, but do not necessarily reflect why and how. A study released in January 2004 by The Media Audit of 85 U.S. metro media markets found that the Internet is not a threat to newspapers and that heavy media users did not abandon other forms of media for the Internet. An executive at Media Audit stated,

> Newspaper Web sites are an extension of the newspaper and add audience to the reach of the printed edition. Also, newspaper Web sites are updated throughout the day, which improves a newspaper's ability to compete with television news programs with up-to-the minute breaking news information. (cited in Greenspan, 2004, par. 2)

In fact in 2002, of an estimated 32 million heavy Internet users, 24.6% spent about 7 hours a week on the net, 25.7 million (19.6%) spent 60 minutes a day reading the newspaper, 27 million (20.6%) watched on average more than 300 minutes a day of TV, and 36 million (27.5%) spent an average of more than 180 minutes daily listening to the radio (Greenspan, 2004).

The longitudinal studies that occur across industries continue to unfold interesting statistics regarding Internet use. Most media companies—whether they are traditional outlets such as newspapers and broadcasters, or entertainment, information, software, and electronic manufacturers—are in search of the best model to provide packaged content to audiences. The Seven Observations of Convergence outlined next serve as a strategy for best practices that content providers can use to assess not only their current practices, but also determine future directions. Identification of an issue or problem within an organization leads to practices that incorporate acceptance, development, and growth.

SEVEN OBSERVATIONS OF CONVERGENCE

There are Seven Observations of Convergence that can be used by media organizations in their efforts to operationalize convergence across business units. They are not mutually exclusive, nor do they require a specific order. They do, however, overlap at different points to advance convergence within organizations. The Seven Observations of Convergence are: (a) communication, (b) commitment, (c) cooperation, (d) compensation, (e) culture, (f) competition, and (g) customer.

Communication is imperative because every individual—from corporate leaders to editors, reporters and other media workers involved in the gathering and distribution of content—must be involved in the ongoing conversations about convergence. Convergence discussions must become a part of the daily vernacular. If an organization is to successfully incorporate convergence, the planning and execution process must center on communication throughout the organization. The driver of a newspaper delivery truck as well as a TV camera operator or a vice president must be capable of articulating the company's convergence objectives and operations.

Commitment is an organization's incorporation of convergence as a part of its mission and philosophy. This is the way the organization conducts business. This argument is more than a top–down initiative, but a commitment that is infused externally and internally through corporate leaders, management, journalists, daily practices, economics, and technology. The economic commitment must be coupled with the support of research and development as well as skill development training (Griffith, Zammuto, & Aiman-Smith, 1999; Smythe, 1999). Such a commitment is evidenced by Media General's The News Center in Tampa, a $40 million "temple" that houses the TV station, newspaper, and online business under one roof.

Cooperation is a necessity for everyone from corporate executives to senior management and frontline workers to operate daily and the process to move forward. Members of news organizations must be open to sharing ideas and news tips and making decisions on how convergence is best operationalized. Cooperation also involves staff from different departments and business units collaboratively working together to develop and execute ideas for content. In convergence operations, print and broadcast journalists are being asked to exchange roles on occasion. For example, a print journalist could conduct a broadcast standup or be interviewed as an expert on air. Broadcast journalists are refining their writing skills to develop copy for print and online units. In a cooperative environment, the advancements of new media are not seen as supplanting traditional media, but offering an alternative for content delivery.

Compensation is a growing concern for journalists, particularly in print, as the organization's demands for more skills and knowledge increase. Media managers must consider how to recognize and reward the additional skills and expertise required of their staff as they evolve. In a digital environment with multimedia delivery of content, journalists and other workers may specialize in one medium, but having an understanding of the multimedia environment is at a premium. Although some media organizations include multimedia initiatives in performance reviews, most managers have not taken any steps to reward these skills monetarily.

Cultural changes within an organization are inevitable and continue to contribute to the acceptance and advancement of convergence in an organization. There are different cultures for individuals who work in print, broadcast, and electronic environments. There is a difference in the language used and methods of production. For nontraditional content providers such as Microsoft and Yahoo, development of information and entertainment content entails understanding how people work in an organization collecting data for simultaneous distribution to a diverse audience. In one example of organizational cultural differences, print journalists have argued that their work brings depth to the printed word and sound bites and electronic clicks are not enough to satiate the needs of readers. Broadcasters recognize the visual nature of society and their ability to capture viewers' attention on TV. The blending of these cultural dynamics is key to the success of convergence within an organization. In most instances, because of the production cycle of print, broadcast and the Internet, some aspects of the culture will remain distinctive in each of these mediums. However, individuals must learn to merge work habits and techniques that have been disparate and competitive or convergence will not be successful.

Competition is approached in different ways in the new media environment. No longer is the competitor just the local print or broadcast franchise; online activities create national and global competition in local markets. *The New York Times* and New York Times Digital now compete with outlets such as Yahoo and the Drudge Report to be the voice of authority on news, information, and entertainment. Traditional media organizations have relied on their reputation as reliable sources of news and information, brand, and credibility. However, new media organizations are making a drive to change the paradigm. Media companies that are practicing convergence through different business subsidiaries must handle local competition both inside and outside the core market. Organizations that do not own other media outlets are seeking to develop partnerships and alliances to maximize their convergence potential.

The *Customer*—audience, reader, viewer, or user—in the new media environment is central to convergence. Despite the interchangeable nature of what term is used, the customer now has more control over which medium he or she chooses to access content. The arguments regarding push-and-pull technology are transformed through use of the computer and the Internet. Companies can no longer merely push the information they want audiences to receive; with the Internet, the customer is in charge and makes the choice to pull only the information he or she selects. Traditional media theories such as gatekeeping have privileged journalists such as editors and news producers as the determinants of the flow of information. In the convergence arena, a transformation has occurred in that relationship, and now customers decide when and what they would like to select for content. The choices are plentiful, ranging from print to radio, TV, cable, cell phones, and the Internet. The segmentation of audiences indicates that people have diverse interests and utilize media in different ways. The challenge for media organizations becomes how to meet those interests and when. Media companies practicing convergence seek to deliver information and entertainment to the platform that is best suited to meet the customer's needs. The real challenge, however, lies in determining what those needs are. During the past several years, many newspapers have switched to a registration process for their online sites, which helps them obtain demographic information about their audience. This effort at demographic profiling provides insight into who is selecting a certain Web site, but does not provide information as to why they selected the site.

The Seven Observations of Convergence have an impact in a variety of ways that can contribute to effective convergence business practices and are applied later in this book using the three convergence pioneers—Tribune Company, Belo, and Media General. The Seven Observations of Convergence are central to the discussion and the research for the case studies of three media conglomerates.

Traditional newspaper readers are distinguished from TV viewing audiences by their desire to have a printed, portable document in hand for perusal. In the era of media convergence, are newspaper audiences now readers or viewers of online content? Do they become users when they interact with content online or remain readers? Do the viewers of broadcast and cable media become multimedia users by accessing information through convergence processes? There is also the issue of competition in convergence. Do the subsidiaries of a media conglomerate remain competitive in a converged environment? If Parent Company A owns TV station B and newspaper C, do those outlets compete?

These are the types of questions that must be answered by organizations that are exploring or have identified convergence as part of the way they do business.

APPROACHES TO CONVERGENCE

Convergence of content within a media organization is still very early in its existence, with little empirical evidence to suggest the best business model. In a multimedia environment, organizations seek to package content in ways that audiences are willing to pay for and receive. To address these convergence issues, this book is organized in two parts. In the first part of the book, chapter 1 focuses on convergence and its numerous definitions, and it provides a brief history and current status of convergence in media organizations using convergence not just as a concept, but a process. Chapter 2 focuses on traditional media organizations and the business practices that these organizations used to adapt to the new media environment. The chapter also examines how conglomeration, convergence, and competition have impacted the industry.

In chapter 3, theoretical implications of emerging digital communication technologies and their impact on the media industry are explored. Rogers' (1995) diffusion of innovations, particularly as it addresses the five stages of the innovation process in organizations, is used to contextualize discussions of media organizations adapting to a new media environment. The chapter profiles the intersection of innovation management research of business and organizational communication to situate the argument on best practices and the importance of viable business models when technology continues to expand delivery choice (Magretta, 2002). The audience is the ultimate determinant of how new media and new media devices such as the Internet, PDAs, and satellite are accepted and adopted. Using media effects research, the uses and gratifications theoretical approach privileges the audience and active selection of media for some use or gratification (Ruggiero, 2000). Uses and gratifications research is used to assess how new media and emerging technologies such as the Internet, wireless, and satellite, in converged organizations, are accessed by audiences.

Part II of the book focuses on the three case studies in chapters 4, 5, and 6, which examine convergence processes from the perspective of three convergence pioneers—Tribune Company, Belo, and Media General. Each organization is comprised of a holding company that includes traditional newspapers, TV stations, cable operations, and Web sites in the same market. The case studies focus on the organizations' media holdings in one market. These media companies were grandfathered in 1975 when the Federal Communications Commission (FCC) initiated the newspaper–broadcast cross-ownership rule. The rule stated that, to maintain diverse voices in a market, one company could not hold a TV and newspaper in the same market; however, newspapers could own broadcast outlets in other markets (Gomery, 2002).

Use of the Internet for presentation of content did not figure into the equation at the time the FCC cross-ownership rule was passed. Media organizations have opposed the rule since its inception. Some thought the 1996 Telecommunications Act, which brought about massive deregulation, would overhaul the cross-ownership rule. The partnerships and alliances that have proliferated in the media industry in recent years have been part of a strategy to address the limits of the FCC rule. The FCC rescinded the cross-ownership rule in a controversial decision on June 2, 2003. Opposition from media advocates such as the Prometheus Radio Project and the Center for Digital Democracy, and conservative groups such as the National Rifle Association and National Council of the Churches of Christ, collaborated and forced a lawsuit in 2003 that was filed in federal district court in Pennsylvania to halt the rule change. In the summer of 2004, the appeals court struck down the changes, and the fate of the FCC cross-ownership rules remain undecided.

Tribune Company is the corporate parent of *The Chicago Tribune*, WGN-TV and radio, CLTV cable, and chicagotribune.com. These are the Chicago-based holdings of the company that purchased Times-Mirror in 2001, which added the top three media markets to its arsenal of operations by including media properties in Los Angeles and New York. The Dallas-based Belo owns *The Dallas Morning News*, WFAA-TV (the ABC affiliate), TXCN statewide,

24-hour cable, and dallasnews.com as part of its media holdings. The Virginia-based Media General owns *The Tampa Tribune*, WFLA-TV (the NBC affiliate), and TBO.com in the Tampa market. Their operations were observed and in-depth interviews conducted with staff and executives from numerous departments to assess how convergence was operationalized and the company's ability to move the process forward in ways other media organizations could not because they were not grandfathered into the FCC's 1975 cross-ownership rule.

Most cities across the country have one major newspaper that is not owned or affiliated with a broadcast outlet. Media groups that do not own multiple media outlets in one market are seeking partnerships with other media organizations to compensate for the changing dynamics in the media industry and to strengthen their positions in various markets. A converged world was developed in Orlando through a partnership between *The Orlando Sentinel* and Time Warner's all-news cable station. The Chicago-based Tribune Co. owns *The Sentinel* and extends the convergence philosophy even if it does not own the local broadcast outlet. Deputy Managing Editor Keith Wheeler argued that research shows one medium helps drive consumers to the other media: "We are no longer just a newspaper. We are a communications company" (cited in Wendland, 2001, par. 19). The staff at *The Sentinel* are becoming multitalented, with reporter/photographers being tagged "VJs or visual journalists" who, with a video camera, are able to capture content for multiple uses (Wendland, 2001). However, media executives such as Stuart Wilk in Dallas caution that, when seeking a partner for convergence, it should be an organization that shares similar values and can manage the cultural differences. Organizational culture has been one of the issues cited as part of the 2003 demise of the AOL and Time Warner convergence merger (Munk, 2004). Although there are benefits in shared resources, there is a cost to convergence, such as the Media General's $40 million building in Tampa, the purchase of new equipment and technology necessary for compatibility of systems, as well as increases in staffing in some instances (Dasbach, 2001). The costs of convergence may not entail the multimillion dollar price tag of a new building, but hiring skilled multimedia staff, on-going training, purchasing new equipment such as digital video cameras for photographers, and sharing costs for resources are a viable part of the equation (Tompkins, 2001). The imperative is that, for convergence to succeed, it takes commitment, financing, and a top–down organizational strategy across all business units of a parent company.

In the concluding chapters, chapter 7 discusses the social, cultural, and political implications of convergence on democracy and the political process. This includes the social responsibility of media organizations in a global environment where, as a result of emerging technologies, the effects of media are enhanced. Chapter 8 addresses the future of convergence with a snapshot of the current concept and process. The visceral nature of the media industry makes it evident that this concluding chapter is the beginning of the ongoing conversation about convergence.

What are we to make of the changing audience in all of these media markets? Individuals no longer access and utilize the media in the way they did just 10 years ago. Newspaper readership penetration is down, and younger audiences—particularly 18- to 30-year-olds—are reportedly not reading newspapers (Compaine, 2000; Dizard, 2000; Newspaper Association of America, 2003). The Internet has become a channel for companies to reach a younger market and niche audiences, rather than a mass appeal. Broadcast news has evolved, with viewers interchanging between cable and network TV outlets. There is intense competition for the public's time and attention. The convergence process is in a stage of evolution, and it is unclear how the final chapter will unfold once the awe and wonder of the Internet, computers, and wireless technology settle and organizations and individuals fall into a cadence with use of new media. However, some studies provide a promising outlook for Internet use and the integration of online and offline properties. In early 2004, the Online Publishers Association found that multi-channel media brands have frequent visitors who feel emotionally attached and equally comfortable with both the on-line and offline entities. The study conducted with Frank N. Magid Associates included 25,852 Internet users between the ages of 18 and 54 on 41 Web sites with a pop-up intercept survey (Online Publishers Association, 2004). The participating Web sites included organizations such as CBS.MarketWatch.com, ChicagoTribune.com, Foodnetwork.com, Bankrate.com, ESPN.com, MercuryNews.com, Style.com, and Weather.com. The study found that of frequent visitors to the 41 Web sites, 72% enjoy the brand's Web site, 71% trust it, 69% look forward to visiting it, and 56% rely on the Web site. Similar figures were reported for the offline properties (Online Publishers Association, 2004).

Although these findings sound promising, this book examines models of convergence in media organizations to assess the current state of convergence and explore trends and ideas for the future. Convergence as a concept and process is in a stage of evolution, and it is unclear how the final chapter will unfold. Research suggests that the uncertainties that lie ahead with emerging digital technologies and their applicability to convergence will impact content providers and the audiences of media and communication technologies for years to come. What is clear is that traditional and new media organizations must continue in their quest for the best practices to integrate new and old media in a converged environment.

REFERENCES

Ball-Rokeach, S. J. (1985). The origins of media systems dependency: A sociological perspective. *Communication Research, 12*(4), 485–510.

Barringer, F. (2001, August 7). Growing audience is turning to established news media [Electronic version]. *The New York Times*. Retrieved February 23, 2002, from http://www.nytimes.com/2001/08/27/business/media/27WEB.html?

Brooks, B. S., Kennedy, G., Moen, D. R., & Ranly, D. (2004). *Telling the story: The convergence of print, broadcast and online media* (2nd ed.). Boston: Bedford/St. Martin's.

Campbell, R. (2000). *Media and culture: An introduction to mass communication* (2nd ed.). Boston, MA: Bedford/St. Martin's.

Carey, J. (2004). The web habit: An ethnographic study of web usage. *Online Publisher's Association White Paper, 2*(1), 1–24. Retrieved January 31, 2004, from http://www.online-publishers.org

Carr, F. (2002, May 2). The tampa model of convergence: Seven levels of co-operation [Electronic Version]. The Poynter Institute. Retrieved July 18, 2002, from http://www.Poynter.org

Compaine, B. M. (2000). The newspaper industry. In B. M. Compaine & D. Gomery (Eds.), *Who owns the media? Competition and concentration in the mass media industry* (3rd ed., pp. 1–60). Mahwah, NJ: Lawrence Erlbaum Associates.

Dasbach, A. (2001). TV and newspaper: Wedded bliss? Special publication of the American Society of Newspaper Editors' Interactive Media Committee. Tampa, FL: *The Tampa Tribune*.

De Sola Pool, I. (1983). *Technologies of freedom.* Cambridge, MA: Belknap Press.

Dizard, W. (2000). *Old media new media: Mass communication in the information age.* New York: Longman.

Fine, J. (2002, April 30). Publishers debate merits of cross-media ownership: Limited gains in ad revenue won't impress Wall Street, exec says. Retrieved April 30, 2002, from http://www.adage.com.

Fredin, E. S., & David, P. (1998). Browsing and the hypermedia interaction cycle: A model of self-efficacy and goal dynamics. *Journalism & Mass Communication Quarterly, 75*(1), 35–54.

Gates, D. (2002, July 10). News sites hustle for profitability. Online Journalism Review. Retrieved July 11, 2002, from http://www.ojr.org/ojr/future/1026348638.php

Gentry, J. (2004). Convergence tracker search page [Electronic Version]. The American Press Institute. Retrieved January 19, 2004, from http://www.americanpressinstitute.org/convergencetracker/search/

Gershon, R. A. (2000). The transnational media corporation: Environmental scanning and strategy formulation. *The Journal of Media Economics, 13*(2), 81–101.

Gomery, D. (2002). *The FCC's newspaper-broadcast cross-ownership rule: An analysis.* Washington, DC: Economic Policy Institute.

Gordon, R. (2003). The meanings and implications of convergence. In K. Kawamoto (Ed.), *Digital journalism: Emerging media and the changing horizons of journalism* (pp. 57–73). Lanham, MD: Rowman & Littlefield.

Greenspan, R. (2004, January 16). Net no threat to newspapers. CyberAtlas. Retrieved January 16, 2004, from http://www.clickz.com/stats/sectors/software/article.php/3300281

Griffith, T. I., Zammuto, R. F., & Aiman-Smith, L. (1999). Why new technologies fail. *Industrial Management, 41*(3), 29–34.

Haiman, R. J. (2001, February 28). Can convergence float? [Electronic Version]. The Poynter Institute. Retrieved January 4, 2005, from http://www.poynter.org/content/content_view.asp?id=14540

Kampinsky, E., Bowman, S., & Willis, C. (2001, November). Amazoning the news: What newspapers can learn from Amazon.com. Special publication of the American Society of Newspaper Editors' Interactive Media Committee. Tampa, FL: *The Tampa Tribune*.

Magretta, J. (2002). Why business models matter. *Harvard Business Review, 80*(5), 86–92.

McLuhan, M. (1997). *Understanding media: The extensions of man.* Cambridge, MA: MIT Press.

Munk, N. (2004). *Fools rush in: Steve Case, Jerry Levin, and the unmaking of AOL Time Warner.* New York: HarperBusiness.

Negroponte, N. (1995). *Being digital.* New York: Vintage Books.

Newspaper Association of America. (2003). *Trends and numbers* [Electronic Version]. Newspaper Association of America. Retrieved June 1, 2003, from http://www.naa.org/artpage.cfm?AID=1610&SID=1022

Online Publishers Association. (2004). Multi-channel media brands: Attitudinal and usage study. Retrieved February 20, 2004, from http://www.online-publishers.org

Pew Internet & American Life Project. (2004, February 29). Content creation online: 44% of U.S. internet users have contributed their thoughts and their files to the online world. Retrieved February 29, 2004, from http://www.pewinternet.org

Rogers, E. M. (1995). *Diffusion of innovations* (4th ed.). New York: The Free Press.

Ruggiero, T. E. (2000). Uses and gratifications theory in the 21st century. *Mass Communication & Society, 3*(1), 3–37.

Schaffer, J. (2001). Convergence: A different view. Special publication of the American Society of Newspaper Editors' Interactive Media Committee. Tampa, FL: *The Tampa Tribune.*

Seib, P. (2001). *Going live.* Lanham, MD: Rowman & Littlefield.

Smythe, D. (1999). Facing the future: Preparing new information professionals. *The Information Management Journal, 33*(2), 44–48.

Steinbock, D. (2000). Building dynamic capabilities: The Wall Street Journal interactive edition: A successful online subscription model (1993–2000) [Electronic Version]. *International Journal of Media Management, 2*(3), 178–194.

Surowiecki, J. (2001). Books will endure, but will publishers? In. K. K. Massey (Ed.), *Readings in mass communication: Media literacy and culture* (2nd ed., pp. 67–69). Boston: McGraw-Hill.

Tompkins, A. (2001, February 28). Convergence needs a leg to stand on [Electronic Version]. The Poynter Institute. Retrieved September 20, 2002, from http://www.poynter.org/ceterpiece/022801tompkins.htm

U.S. Department of Commerce. (2002). *A nation online: How Americans are expanding their use of the internet.* Washington, DC: Author.

Wendland, M. (2001, February, 26). Convergence: Repurposing journalism [Electronic Version]. The Poynter Institute. Retrieved September 20, 2002, from http://www.poynter.org/ceterpiece/022601.htm

Wirtz, B. W. (1999). Convergence processes, value constellations and integration strategies in the multimedia business. *International Journal of Media Management, 1*(1), 14–22.

2

Traditional Media
and Business Practices

Any discussion of the media should include issues of economics (Gomery, 1989) as well as the media's role in American society as the fourth estate—watchdog of government and policymakers of the administrative, judicial, and legislative estates. Economic issues include the internal structure of a media organization to its economic and performance strategies. Traditional media organizations have relied on their historical exigencies as gatherers and disseminators of information for the public to identify the sources of credible and reliable information on matters of the public interest. Emerging digital technologies in communication and media have changed that paradigm, forcing numerous media organizations to view themselves as content providers of news, information, entertainment, and media products that will attract the largest number of audiences.

This chapter addresses basic concepts, terms, and trends that are fundamental to understanding the trends in media concentration, mergers and acquisitions, as well as business practices relevant to convergence. The economic terms and practices identified are used by the media industry in the development and dissemination of their product. The evolution of books, newspapers, magazines, radio, TV, cable, and the Internet in the era of convergence and emerging technologies is applicable to the roles each medium plays in today's environment. The concept of the marketplace of ideas is explored to explicate issues of the democratic process being impacted by fewer owners of media outlets controlling the news and information that flows to the public. The policy-related issues that are relevant to the media industry influence some of the performance and operational strategies of the media. All of these elements converge as media companies continue exploring the best business practices for the expansion of their products.

INDUSTRY CHANGES

As the growth and global expansion of the media industry escalated, corporate leaders used mergers and acquisitions as a vehicle to approach the change. The 2004 *State of the News Media* released by the Project for Excellence in Journalism found that overall the media industry was doing better than expected. For example, newspaper ad revenues increased 60% between 1991 and 2000, with profits up by 207% (Saba, 2004). This may speak to why, over the years, mergers and acquisitions, the blending of assets and capital for the purpose of growth (Ozanich & Wirth, 1998), have played such a prominent role across the media industry. The type and extent of that growth is based on the goals of individual media organizations. Determining which media entities to merge or acquire is a systematic process that individual organizations must assess to have a successful union. More than 10 years ago, Disney CEO Michael Eisner stated that a merger was a growth option for his company based on economic and business strategies, as well as his previous professional experience with the ABC network (The Walt Disney Company, 1995). In the company's annual report, Eisner foreshadowed the Capital Cities/ABC merger as key to the future of the organization. Other media leaders follow a similar approach when trying to determine whether a merger or acquisition is the next step for their organization. This line of reasoning is also used to examine issues such as similar products, markets, financial status, growth, product development, or capturing the new media market by establishing a site for Internet content (Compaine & Gomery, 2000; Higgins, 1999).

For an organization to set up a merger or acquisition, internal and external decision making occurs on several levels. There are three phases in this process: (a) planning, (b) transaction, and (c) implementation (Ozanich & Wirth, 1998). In the *planning phase*, an organization assesses its long-term goals and corporate plans and strategies. Decisions are made on which companies to target and their market valuation. An example of this stage, although it was problematic in its implementation, can be found in the AOL/Time Warner merger announced in January 2000. AOL, with CEO Steve Case, was the upstart new media company of the late 20th century. Case wanted to strengthen his company's position as an Internet service provider by aligning with CEO Gerald Levin's established media and entertainment giant Time Warner. At the time of the history-making merger announcement, the market capitalization of AOL was $164 billion to Time Warner's $83 billion (Munk, 2004). Many considered AOL's worth grossly over-inflated and not a merger of equals because the recorded revenue the year before was $4.8 billion for AOL and $27 billion for Time Warner. Case and Levin, however, were determined to pursue their dream of an "Internet-driven media entertainment company" (p. 143). More is discussed later on the AOL/Time Warner deal and the fallout of this merger and acquisition, but here it illustrates how one company may view another as economically attractive for expansion.

The *transaction phase* occurs when the organization targets a company for acquisition and makes plans to structure the deal. The deal could be a mutual or hostile takeover (e.g., Comcast's hostile bid for Disney in 2004). The deal could be structured as stock, cash, or a combination including percentage of ownership (e.g., GE's merger with Vivendi Universal in 2004). At the *implementation phase*, the merger or acquisition is in process, and the necessary steps are enacted for the structure of the deal and any external regulatory approvals that might exist (Ozanich & Wirth, 1998). The process must also take into account shareholders when the company is a publicly held entity. For example, not only did the Disney board oppose Comcast's hostile bid, but a verbose group of shareholders reiterated the same at the annual meeting on March 3, 2004. Media executives have a fiduciary responsibility to align the organization in financially sound enterprises. Comcast officials eventually withdrew their bid, but the potential for converging the cable giant and the movie studio could have created new forms of content delivery.

Mergers and acquisitions are an in-depth process encompassing a range of internal and external factors that corporate leaders must consider. Mergers and acquisitions can be either vertical and horizontal mergers or conglomeration. Vertical integration occurs when a company has control of the product from the initial idea to producing and distributing the final product. Horizontal integration is a company owning similar businesses as part of its strategy for growth. Conglomeration occurs when a large company such as GE owns different industries from appliances to industrial to NBC Universal TV and movie studio.

IDEAS IN THE MARKETPLACE

The potential reduction of multiple voices in the media arena and a reduction of ideas in the marketplace are extensions of the argument against synergistic behavior and concentrated ownership of media outlets. The increase in public affairs knowledge is one of the premises of the *marketplace of ideas* metaphor. The founders of this country decided that a free press—print only at that time—would be the vehicle to best inform that public. Thus, we received the amendments to the U.S. Constitution, with the First Amendment being the often-quoted repertoire of the media. A stronger democracy is created, enhanced, and maintained by everyone having access to information pertinent to the democratic process and the growth of society (Bagdikian, 1997; McChesney, 1999). Scholars, government, and policymakers have consistently identified the need for media to serve the public good. However, in the midst of all the media consolidation, critics contend that the idea of a marketplace of ideas for the public is losing ground.

The media should promote a free flow of ideas and information in society. Media mergers and acquisitions matter because of the potential threat to the free flow of ideas in the marketplace. Critics contend that, with concentrated media ownership, the watchdog role may be compromised when the trail of discovery leads to a parent company (Conrad, 1997). Fruitful discussion could be raised from various vantage points on the *Los Angeles Times* winning five Pulitzer Prizes in 2004 despite that its parent company, Times Mirror, was purchased by Tribune Company in 2000. Tribune's purchase resulted in a gain of print, broadcasting, and online prominence in the top three markets of Los Angeles, Chicago, and New York. Some might suggest that *The Times'* editorial voices were not limited because the multiple winning of journalism's top prize might reflect that big media and synergistic behavior is not necessarily the death knell for a diversity of voices in the marketplace. Perhaps in this age of concentration and convergence, "The issue isn't who owns the media; it's what those owners do with it" (Kolodzy, 2003, par. 1) that will determine the good and bad of concentration and convergence.

The marketplace of ideas metaphor has been interpreted from both democratic and economic theory perspectives. Economic-based interpretations focus on efficiency, consumer satisfaction, and competition. Democratic-based theory looks more at citizen knowledge, informed decision making, and effective self-government (Napoli, 1999a). From an economic theory perspective, arguments are against government regulation of media and allow the market to dictate the needs of the industry. This is where the 1996 Telecommunications Act's deregulation of the industry facilitated more exchanges and deals among media companies in various markets. From a democratic perspective, there is a call for regulation to maintain the media's role as serving in the best interest of the public. Too much deregulation may allow media to lose its focus and not keep the public interest at the forefront. Scholars, media executives, advocates, and the public continue to debate which theoretical perspective best meets the needs of the public.

Napoli (1999b) took the ideas of multiple voices in the marketplace another step by examining the diversity principle as it relates to communications policy and a range of voices in the marketplace. The FCC contends that maintaining diversity, localism, and competition is the focus of the agency's actions. On the matter of media diversity, Napoli (1999b) identified three components: source, content, and exposure diversity. The complex structure of the media industry across media outlets, corporate holdings, and international borders is conducive to such an approach.

Source diversity is implicit in the marketplace of ideas metaphor because numerous outlets are expected to provide a more abundant supply of information to the public. Policymakers look at source diversity as a mixture of ownership in content or programming, diversity of individuals who own media outlets, and diversity in the workforce employed by media.

Content diversity follows source diversity in that more diverse content should be provided with multiple owners or originators of content. Falling under the rubric of content diversity would be program type, meaning numerous offerings of programs and messages to meet a variety of interests. The goal is access to free and diverse medium systems as information sources. Examples include cable, direct broadcast satellite (DBS), wireless communications, radio, print, or Internet access.

Exposure diversity is defined as access to different types of media by the public. Napoli (1999b) defined horizontal exposure diversity as the way audiences distribute themselves across different content options (e.g., Internet, cable, TV, or print). Vertical exposure occurs when audiences are polarized to extremes in consuming or avoiding some media.

Table 2.1 clarifies the connections among source, content, and exposure diversity and their subcomponents as they relate to the

TABLE 2.1
Diversity Components, Subcomponents,
and Assumed Relationships

Source Diversity	Content Diversity	Exposure Diversity
1. Ownership	1. Program type or format	1. Horizontal
a. programming	2. Demographic	2. Vertical
b. outlet	3. Idea-viewpoint	
2. Workforce		

Source: Napoli, P. (1999b). Deconstructing the diversity principle. *Journal of Communication, 49*(4), 10. Reprinted with permission by Philip M. Napoli.

ideas of diversity in communication policy (Napoli, 1999b). Napoli's approach is illustrative of the types of connections and numerous entry points for news and information to be distributed by the media to serve the public welfare. My arguments incorporate a more proactive role for the public, which adds the dynamic of interactivity and participation in the exchange of news, information, and entertainment media.

In a concentrated media environment, the issue is not whether audiences access the material, but that a diverse body of news and information is readily available from multiple sources. Priorities in public affairs knowledge must focus on keeping a multiplicity of news, information, and entertainment choices regardless of the sources. Also, the public in this information age is charged with being proactive in acknowledging, accessing, and understanding the sources and owners of the content they access.

The axiom "follow the money" is used in journalism schools when discussions arise on how to investigate questions of corruption or malfeasance. The paradigm has shifted for the public as well, which will not only have to follow the money, but the source of the content and the ownership trail of the media outlet. This begs for more discussion on media literacy in the new millennium, with emerging digital technologies impacting communication and media. Media literacy is an important and substantive conversation that should not be neglected. When a movie theater darkens and the credits role, the curiosity of the public should reach beyond who starred in or directed the movie to the producer and distributor of the film, overseas distribution, and its byproducts. Reading the newspaper or a magazine should include interest in not only the articles and photographs, but the writers, editors, publishers, and owners of the publication, as well as the parent company.

Another approach to the discussion of the marketplace of ideas breaks the diversity of media ideas into two areas: diversity of ideas and diversity of products (Iosifides, 1999). Diversity of ideas includes a number of choices for the public in programs and media outlets as sources of information. Content should be accessible to all of the public and provide a variety of choices. Diversity of product translates to a range in the types of products offered. Media

owners would provide numerous media channels from TV and cable to radio and newspapers. The public would benefit from the
technological developments and the access to improved and
economical communication choices.

The concept of a free marketplace of ideas is forced to play
against the lucrative nature of the building block effect of media
concentration. Journalists are concerned with the impact of corporate ownership on the editorial product. Many have become disaf-
fected and defected from the ranks of daily journalism. Some
journalists worry that hard work and good journalism will be lost
in the maze of corporate bottom lines (McManus, 1994). The very
nature of the corporate structure of media organizations creates a
hierarchy where front-line employees such as reporters and photographers report to editors, managers, producers, and news division heads. The higher up in the corporate media leadership food
chain, the greater the expectation that economic efficiency and cost
savings are the mantra. Critics worry that managing some economic losses to increase spending on investigative projects or
costly news bureaus in foreign lands is shunned. Preserving
democracy through an informed public becomes difficult in media
corporations that place less emphasis on a diversity of voices providing information to the public. The marketplace of ideas is
threatened by such organizations. The increase in media concentration challenges media owners to make a profit while providing a
multiplicity of media voices. Critics such as McChesney (1999) and
Bagdikian (2004) suggested that this is not occurring in a concentrated media environment, and their arguments cannot go unan-
swered. If media convergence in a concentrated environment is to
be a success, then media executives must articulate to the public
how their needs and expectations will not only be met, but expanded due to the opportunities provided by emerging technologies for gathering and disseminating content.

REGULATION

The era of media concentration did not start with headlines of billion dollar mergers and acquisitions. It has been a process that in-

cluded regulatory, economic, and industry changes. Media companies were mostly family owned or other private ownership arrangements until the 1960s, when many companies started to sell their stock publicly. By the 1980s, mergers and acquisitions were off and running in broadcast and print industries. Deregulation contributed to media concentration as the political/economic climate during the Reagan/Bush administrations in the 1980s moved away from government regulation to encourage a marketplace approach to the media industry (Fowler & Brenner, 1982). By the time the FCC approved the 1996 Telecommunications Act, a floodgate was opened that many policymakers and legislators thought would create more competition in media through the convergence of phone companies, cable, and traditional media. Instead it has resulted in more concentration.

The large, multibillion-dollar media deals such as Disney/ABC, Viacom/CBS, and AOL/Time Warner were widely publicized because of the sheer size and costs of the deals. Compaine (2000) asserted that concentration of media ownership in the hands of a few should be clarified. He found that most media holdings either fall under the category of founders and their descendants (e.g., Rupert Murdoch and News Corp. or Sumner Redstone and Viacom) or a number of large institutional investment groups (e.g., Time Warner or Gannett) seeking long-term profits and increased value from proven performance.

Journalists, the public, scholars, and others usually do not focus on the economic viability of media organizations, but corporate executives are driven by the bottom line. By the 1990s, working journalists found that market-driven initiatives became more a part of their lives than many of them wanted to entertain. With media concentration came corporate executives with agendas that might be separate from those of working journalists. The challenge lies in how to get both parties to the same conclusion when they have opposite perspectives. In *Market Driven Journalism*, McManus (1994) addressed issues that developed as media concentration proliferated and journalists felt shut out and forced into formulaic, nonthreatening reporting on government, politicians, and business leaders. Big corporate leaders do not want lengthy and costly lawsuits, but much of good journalism falls into comforting the afflicted and afflicting the comforted. For example, there was the *60 Minutes* debacle in 1995 involving the tobacco company whistleblower in which the CBS lawyers and corporate honchos decided to sit on correspondent Mike Wallace's exclusive interview. The story was eventually reported by *The New York Times* and *The Wall Street Journal* and resulted in a movie, *The Insider*, which brought attention inside and outside of the industry on the potential of corporate leaders to impact journalistic practices.

The FCC regulation of the broadcast industry dates to The Communications Act of 1934, which sought to obtain the most benefit out of radio for the public by limiting ownership of the medium by broadcasting chains. Unlike newspaper publishers, who are protected under the U.S. Constitution's First Amendment, the airwaves belong to the public, and broadcasting is a privilege granted by a license to operate from the federal government. More than 60 years later, the 1996 Telecommunications Act changed the playing field for media by deregulating the industry and creating new avenues for change. The Act removed restrictions on the national TV station ownership from a cap of 12 to no more than 35% of U.S. TV-viewing households. The regulatory changes also included an increase in the number of radio stations a company can own, an increase in the broadcast license renewal period from 4 to 8 years, and allowance of common ownership of cable systems and broadcast networks.

Although deregulation after the 1996 Act prompted a lot of activity in the industry, the FCC newspaper/broadcast cross-ownership ban was still in effect. Cross-ownership of newspapers and broadcast outlets in the same market has been barred since 1975 unless the organization was a grandfathered arrangement that existed prior to regulations (e.g., the three convergence pioneers discussed in this book: Tribune Company, Belo, and Media General). The FCC's vote to lift the ban in 2003 was stayed by a federal court. Until this regulatory hurdle changes, the convergence pioneers discussed in this book serve as an example of the potential for convergence if print, broadcast, and online platforms are owned by one company in the same market. Convergence presents different strategies for companies, but the resulting benefits for media, content, working journalists, technology, and the economics continue to be examined.

TECHNOLOGY, CONVERGENCE, FOREIGN COMPETITION

Several factors have been reported as contributing to media growth and concentration. The obvious one is technology. The rise in emerging digital technologies has reconfigured the platforms for content delivery. The ability to condense information digitally and move it through more channels presents new opportunities to reach different audiences. The growth in cable, the Internet, and wireless technologies has enabled companies to reach larger audiences, digital transmission of data, and potential increases in broadband width, providing more channels and gateways to media.

For national security, foreign governments, companies, and individuals cannot own more than 25% of a U.S. broadcast property unless they receive a waiver, according to Section 310 (b) (4) of the Communications Act of 1934 (Foreign Ownership Guidelines, 2004). In 1986, Australian Rupert Murdoch obtained American citizenship to avoid a fight with the FCC over ownership of the FOX network by a foreigner. The FOX network broke the stronghold that the Big Three networks—ABC, CBS, and NBC—had had on the broadcasting industry since the 1950s. Murdoch continues to be a key player in the concentrated media industry, with his 2003 purchase of DirecTV from Hughes Corp. and his plans to aggressively move to interactive TV.

Murdoch also announced in 2004 that he would move the corporate headquarters of News Corp. from Australia to the United States. He is the epitome of a media mogul in a concentrated environment, much to the consternation and distraction of media titans such as Ted Turner, Michael Eisner, and Barry Diller. Murdoch's strategies for the different markets he serves, as well as his use of technology, convergence, and synergistic behavior, are well documented. Murdoch's purchase of DirecTV moved him into a new stratosphere with lofty ideas for use of his satellite network. DirecTV is one of the top two players; the other is Echo Star's Dish Network, which provides satellite service in the United States. Murdoch already owns BSkyB satellite network in the U.K. and Asia, offering interactivity capabilities on TV from gambling to sports and connectivity to food and retail industries. U.S. media executives are wary of Murdoch's competitive edge and ponder the media products and services they must offer, in addition to content, to remain competitive.

Table 2.2 is adapted from a graphic in *The New York Times* (Ink and Airwaves, 2003) that illustrates convergence possibilities for companies that own print and broadcast outlets in the same market.

Regulation weaknesses can be seen in Tribune Company's purchase of Times Mirror. The merger deal will not be considered by the FCC before 2006 because Times Mirror does not hold any renewable broadcast licenses, and Tribune Company's broadcast licenses are not up for review until that time (Albiniak, 2000). Despite consolidation concerns and the role of the public interest, the new legislation (1996 Telecommunications Act) enshrines the idea of competition as "the key to media progress in the coming century" (Pavlik, 1996, p. 35).

The battleground has been prepped for a new debate with the FCC's June 2, 2003, relaxing of several regulations that critics argue increase the potential for even more consolidation. The new rules allow cross-ownership of newspapers and TVs in the same market, potential TV duopolies and triopolies, and ownership of TV stations that reach 45% of the market—up from 35%. Controversy over the FCC rule changes erupted in the summer of 2003, and a federal lawsuit was filed in a Pennsylvania court to halt the changes. The lawsuit was spurred by an unlikely collaboration of allies such as the Prometheus Radio Project, Center for Digital Democracy and Fairness and Accuracy in Reporting, and the Civil Rights Forum on Communications Policy, as well as numerous prominent media organizations that support removing the ban (Prometheus Radio Project v. Federal Communications Commission, 2004). The federal court rejected the FCC rule changes in the summer of 2004. Supporters of the changes, such as media com-

TABLE 2.2
Converged Media Markets

MEDIA	MARKET	NEWSPAPER	TV STATION
Tribune	New York	Newsday	WPIX (WB)
	Los Angeles	Los Angeles Times	KTLA (WB)
	Chicago	**Chicago Tribune**	**WGN (WB), CLTV cable, WGN radio, chicagotribune.com**
	Hartford, CT	Hartford Courant	WTIC (Fox)
			WTXX (WB)
	Miami/ Ft. Lauderdale	South Florida Sun Sentinel	WBZL (WB)
News Corp.	New York	New York Post	WNYW (Fox)
Belo	**Dallas**	**Dallas Morning News**	**WFAA (ABC), TXCN cable, dallasnews.com**
Cox	Atlanta	Atlanta Journal-Constitution	WSB (ABC)
Media General	**Tampa, FL**	**Tampa Tribune**	**WFLA (NBC), TBO.com**
Gannett	Phoenix	Arizona Republic	KPNX (NBC)
	Grand Rapids Kalamazoo/Battle Creek, MI	Battle Creek Enquirer	WZZM (ABC)
E. W. Scripps	Cincinnati, OH	Cincinnati Post	WCPO (ABC)
	West Palm Beach, Ft. Pierce, FL	Ft. Pierce Tribune	WPTV (NBC)

Source: Ink and airwaves. (2003, May 25). *The New York Times* [Electronic Version]. http://www.nytimes.com. Reprinted with permission by *The New York Times*.

panies and FCC Chair Michael Powell, as well as detractors, argue the case may end up before the U.S. Supreme Court. Criticism of deregulation centers on media ownership and the future of the media industry as a result of relaxed regulation and the marketplace as a determinant of change, competition, and diverse ideas.

CONCLUSION

A series of competing economic and management issues historically and currently in the media industry influence the performance and operations of media companies. This book includes numerous examples of media consolidation and conglomeration, and it closely examines three media companies that are pioneers in promoting convergence. The issues include not just ownership of multiple media, but operation of different media outlets, corporate performance, profits, corporate responsibility, influence of convergence and emerging technologies, and continued contributions to the free flow of ideas in the marketplace. Chapter 3 examines theoretical issues salient to concentrated media ownership and emerging technologies. Discussion includes integration of Rogers' diffusion theory as it relates to adoption of new technologies and changes in organizations. Also from business and communication research, the innovation process in organizations is explored for issues relevant to media companies. The organizational perspective is fused with the audience and end user's perspective by utilizing uses and gratifications research to explicate media choices by individuals with some motive and gratification being sought or obtained.

REFERENCES

Albiniak, P. (2000). It's almost as if there's no rule: Crossownership from $6.5b merger won't matter until at least 2006; by then lobbyists think FCC will scrap regs. *Broadcasting & Cable, 130*(12), 8–9.

Bagdikian, B. H. (1997). *The media monopoly* (5th ed.). Boston: Beacon.

Bagdikian, B. H. (2004). *The new media monopoly.* Boston: Beacon.

Compaine, B. M. (2000). Who owns the media companies? In B. M. Compaine & D. Gomery, *Who owns the media?* (3rd ed., pp. 481–506). Mahwah, NJ: Lawrence Erlbaum Associates.

Compaine, B. M., & Gomery, D. (2000). *Who owns the media?* (3rd ed.). Mahwah, NJ: Lawrence Erlbaum Associates.

Conrad, K. (1997, April). Media merger: First step in a new shift of antitrust analysis? *Federal Communications Law Journal.* Retrieved November 1, 1999, from Lexis-Nexis Academic Universe.

Foreign Ownership Guidelines. (2004). Foreign ownership guidelines for FCC common carrier and aeronautical radio licenses: Section 310 of the communications act of 1934 as amended. International Bureau, Federal Communications Commission. Retrieved December 5, 2004, from http://hraunfoss.fcc.gov/edocs_public/attachmatch/DA-04-3610A2.pdf

Fowler, M. S., & Brenner, D. L. (1982). A marketplace approach to broadcast regulation. *Texas Law Review, 60*(2), 207–257.

Gomery, D. (1989). Media economics: Terms of analysis. *Critical Studies in Mass Communication, 6,* 43–60.

Higgins, J. M. (1999). The next "big deal": Media companies are still in a merger mood. *Broadcasting and Cable, 129*(7), 30–31.

Ink and Airwaves. (2003, May 25). *The New York Times* [Electronic Version]. Retrieved, May 26, 2003, from http://www.nytimes.com

Iosifides, P. (1999). Diversity versus concentration in the deregulated mass media domain. *Journalism & Mass Communication Quarterly, 76*(1), 151–162.

Kolodzy, J. (2003). Media convergence is an opportunity, not a curse. *Columbia Journalism Review, 4* [Electronic Version]. Retrieved January 14, 2004, from http://www.cjr.org/issues/2003/4/voices-kolodzy.asp?

McChesney, R. W. (1999). *Rich media poor democracy.* Urbana, IL: University of Illinois Press.

McManus, J. (1994). *Market-driven journalism: Let the citizen beware.* Thousand Oaks, CA: Sage.

Munk, N. (2004). *Fools rush in: Steve Case, Jerry Levin, and the unmaking of AOL Time Warner.* New York: HarperBusiness.

Napoli, P. (1999a). The marketplace of ideas metaphor in communications regulation. *Journal of Communication, 49*(4), 151–169.

Napoli, P. (1999b). Deconstructing the diversity principle. *Journal of Communication, 49*(4), 7–34.

Ozanich, G. W., & Wirth, M. O. (1998). Mergers and acquisitions: A communications industry overview. In A. Alexander, J. Owers, & R. Carveth (Eds.), *Media economics: Theory and practice* (2nd ed., pp. 95–107). Mahwah, NJ: Lawrence Erlbaum Associates.

Pavlik, J. V. (1996). Competition: Key to the communications future? *Television Quarterly, 28*(2), 35–42.

Prometheus Radio Project v. Federal Communications Commission, 373 F.3d 372 (3rd Cir. 2004).

Saba, J. (2004). Study raises questions about profit/circ link. *Editor & Publisher 137*(4), 9.

The Walt Disney Company. (1995). *Annual report.* Burbank, CA: Author.

3

Theoretical Implications

As communication technologies enter our world, the adoption rate for use and length of stay varies, the expectations and needs of audiences shift over time, and the factors that contribute to use are inconsistent in determining whether the market adopts the device. In the annals of failed technologies, the eight-track tape lived a short life. The same is true of several communication and media technologies: Atira game players, videotext, viewtron, and Beta versions of videotapes (Carlson, 2003; Dizard, 2000; Kawamato, 2003). Rogers' (1995) seminal work, *Diffusion of Innovations*, has been used in numerous industries as a theoretical foundation to examine how new innovations or ideas are adopted.

Historically, as new media devices are developed, users adapt in various ways according to a need that may be met or satisfied. According to Rogers (1995), individuals usually adapt to a new technology based on issues such as the new device has more advantages than the device it replaces, how difficult the device is to use, and whether the results of the use of the device can be observed by others. From an audience perspective, media organizations must assess how to meet their interests in an electronic environment. From an organizational perspective, for purposes of discussion of convergence as both a concept and process we use, Rogers' (1995) five stages of the innovation process in organizations: (a) agenda setting, (b) matching, (c) redefining/restructuring, (d) clarifying, and (e) routinizing. Rogers' innovation process for organizations is salient to media organizations that incorporate convergence as part of their business practices. In this chapter, we explore how Rogers' five stages of the innovation process in organizations impact media companies as they seek to cope with emerging digital technologies in the demanding 24-hour, 7-days-a-week, 365-days-a-year media industry with intense competition and content challenges. Challenges include development of multimedia content that either complement or supplement established brick-and-mortar offerings, sharing of content and resources across platforms, or partnerships and affiliations with different media outlets. We also discuss surveys that have identified multi-use trends and habits of media users on- and offline that contribute to the new expectations in the industry.

INTERNET EXPLOSION

Media organizations rushed to the Internet in the 1990s to develop a presence online. For example, at many newspapers, most online versions were replicas of the print version through the use of shovelware, which takes printed material and "shovels" its duplicate online without catering the content to the new medium. This process was short-lived, and Rogers' suggestions on innovation adoption are applicable to stages of acceptance of the Internet and other emerging technologies by media. In Table 3.1, Rogers' (1995) five stages of the innovation process in an organization are illustrated to examine their applicability to media organizations.

In organizations, the innovation process includes two broad activities: *initiation*, defined as "all of the information gathering, conceptualizing and planning for the adoption of an innovation, leading up to the decision to adopt," and *implementation*, defined as "all of the events, actions, and decisions involved in putting an innovation into use" (Rogers, 1995, p. 392). Initiation incorporates agenda setting and matching, then a decision is made on the innovation and events move to implementation, which includes redefining/restructuring, clarifying, and routinizing.

The stages of the innovation process in an organization incorporate the movement of an innovation into an organization's cultural norms. The first stage, agenda setting, occurs when an important issue or problem is placed in front of the organization; matching occurs when the problem is matched with an innovation likely to

TABLE 3.1
The Innovation Process in an Organization

	Decision			
I. INITIATION		II. IMPLEMENTATION		
#1	#2	#3	#4	#5
AGENDA SETTING	MATCHING	REDEFINING/ RESTRUCTURING	CLARIFYING	ROUTINIZING
General organizational problems that may create a perceived need for innovation.	Fitting a problem from the organization's agenda with an innovation.	The innovation is modified and reinvented to fit the organization, and organizational structures are altered.	The relationship between the organization and the innovation is defined more clearly.	The innovation becomes an ongoing element in the organization's activities and loses its identity.

Note. Reprinted with the permission of The Free Press, a Division of Simon & Schuster Adult Publishing Group, from *Diffusions of Innovations*, 4th ed. By Everett M. Rogers. Copyright © 1995 by Everett M. Rogers, Copyright © 1962, 1971, 1983 by The Free Press. All rights reserved.

solve the issue; and redefining/restructuring occurs when the innovation is modified and reinvented to fit the organization's situation. At the clarifying stage, the relationship between the innovation and organization is more clearly defined as it is placed in full and regular use, and at routinizing the innovation loses its separate identity. Let us take a closer look at the five stages of the innovation process in organizations as posited by Rogers (1995).

AGENDA SETTING

Rogers' theoretical arguments are applicable to the media at the agenda-setting stage when media organizations recognized the influence of emerging technologies on the industry with the increased use of the Internet, growth of PC usage, and ensuing implications. Internally, in many newsrooms during the early 1990s, access to the Internet at workstations was not widespread; in the world of computer-assisted reporting today, it is the norm. Early on, working journalists were often given access to the Web through a hierarchy of need and job function. Media companies used their in house intranets for e-mail communication among the staff. This became problematic in newsrooms of all types as the Internet increased the distribution cycle of news, information, and entertainment. To function effectively, it became apparent to news managers that everyone must have access to the Internet to perform their jobs. This author recalls requirements to read daily not only the paper at which she worked, but two to three competing entities. With the rise of the Internet, the competition was no longer local, statewide, and regional, but national and international. Access to all types of information through numerous channels was essential.

Outside the walls of a media organization, whether print or broadcast, news or entertainment, information or commerce, the public was accessing the Internet at any time, at any place, and for a multitude of reasons. Here is where the media industry recognized that new ways of connecting (pardon the pun) to readers and viewers were necessary to remain a viable commodity in the lives of busy users and readers. The first entree on the Internet for many media organizations was through Internet portals such as Prodigy or AOL in the early 1990s. Media organizations later moved away from portal use for access to the Web. The following mini case study provides an example of how going directly to the Internet with an online site was born out of necessity and innovation.

Mini Case Study: The Detroit News

The Detroit News and *The Detroit Free Press* are two large metropolitan dailies that are identified here to illustrate how and why the industry environment in the mid-1990s necessitated *The Detroit News* skipping the step of an Internet portal and going directly to the Web.

The Detroit News has been a staple in Detroit since its inception in 1873. *The News* was viewed as a conservative newspaper, independently owned by the Evening News Association, until it was purchased by the Gannett Co. in 1985. *The News* had been in a long-standing circulation and advertising battle with the *Detroit Free Press* to win the local market. The tactics used by both newspapers included reduced newsstand prices, home delivery discounts, advertising rate reductions, and beefed-up editorial operations. Newsstand rates for the newspapers were among the lowest around the country—at 15 cents for *The News* and 20 cents for the *Free Press* when other newspapers' daily cost had increased to 50 cents and $1 by the 1980s and 1990s (Gonyea & Hoyt, 1997).

The newspaper war ceased in 1989 when *The Detroit News* entered into a controversial joint operating agreement (JOA) with long-time rival the *Detroit Free Press* to form the Detroit Newspaper Agency (Gonyea & Hoyt, 1997). The papers applied for the JOA by listing the *Free Press* as the failing newspaper. At the time of the JOA application, *The News* was predicted to lose $11.5 million and the Free Press $9 million ("Detroit Newspaper," 1985). The newspaper owners touted the JOA as an opportunity to preserve two editorial voices in Detroit. There was staunch opposition to the JOA from advertisers, the community, state legislators, the media industry, and many others. Once the JOA was approved, it was predicted that the two newspapers would stabilize and eventually become financially solvent. The Detroit Newspaper Agency did not post a profit after the JOA until 1994 (Gonyea & Hoyt, 1997). *The News* and *Free Press* were numbers 9 and 10, respectively, in national circulation in 1989. To compound the situation, unions struck the papers in 1995. Almost 10 years later, in 1997, *The News* had dropped in circulation to number 43 and the *Free Press* to number 21, and in 2000 *The News* and *Free Press* were numbers 44 and 21, respectively (Editor & Publisher, 2001; Gonyea & Hoyt, 1997). The circulation decline from the time of the strike has yet to be recouped.

Detnews.com

The newspaper industry has struggled with circulation and advertising losses for some time, escalating by the 1990s to more financial losses and newspaper closings. The 1995 Detroit newspaper strike did not stop either newspaper from publishing. In addition to management, replacement workers, and strikers who eventually crossed the picket line, technology contributed significantly to keeping the Detroit newspapers publishing. The infrastructure for an online operation provided *The Detroit News* the means to distribute its content electronically during the strike.

Before the strike, executives at *The News* had planned to launch detnews.com because a previous decision had been made to go straight to the Internet. Those plans were accelerated the day the newspaper strike began on July 13, 1995. According to Nancy Malitz, Assistant Managing Editor/New Media for *The News*, for more than 18 months prior to the strike, management at *The News* had been analyzing what method to use to launch its online version of the newspaper. Two business models were considered that were prominent for online operations in the early 1990s. First, the AOL or Prodigy arrangement for a fee or percentage was considered with *The News* linking up with one of the Internet service providers (ISP) to offer the newspaper online. *The Chicago Tribune* had such an arrangement with AOL, with a 6% ownership in the ISP before launching chicagotribune.com. Second, a sign-up or subscription fee similar to *The Wall Street Journal Interactive* subscription model was considered. The newspaper management even considered getting into the ISP business, but abandoned that approach. According to Malitz, it became apparent to management at *The News* that, with emerging technologies, they were no longer just a newspaper, but a content provider competing across multiple platforms.

MATCHING

Media organizations reach the *matching stage* by developing online divisions with staff and resources within the organization or as separate business units. The Detroit News Agency is one example of this process, but there are many. In 2001, for example, *The New York Times* celebrated 5 years of *New York Times Digital*, its online sister electronic publication. The occasion was noteworthy because the venerable *Times*, which, with its "all the news that's fit to print" slogan, had long stated no horoscopes, comics, or color for its pages to exemplify its high journalistic standards, but could not argue with the power of new media. Thus, we now have nytimes.com as an alternative delivery channel. The road to the current online presence is covered in some detail with a link at nytimes.com. However, here we discuss the highlights of nytimes.com and the significance of its presence in the online world of news and information. The Web site is applicable to discussions of the matching stage because its creation is a response to the agenda that was set in the public and media industry as computer and Internet use escalated.

What are some of the benefits of developing nytimes.com as Web site that complements its offline counterpart as well as brand recognition in the electronic world? First, nytimes.com consistently ranks among the top news Web sites visited in numerous online and offline surveys of the industry (Multi-Channel Media Brands, 2004; Newspapers, 2004). Second, the Web site has allowed *The Times* to create and distribute information in innovative ways. An example would be *The Times'* electronic publication of the stories of the victims of 9/11 at the World Trade Center. The *Portraits of Grief* series transformed the storytelling process in the journalistic world to one that was simultaneously electronic and printable, but, most important, interactive for those who accessed the site. The infinite capacity of the Internet makes it suitable for providing more of a dynamic experience to both on- and offline audiences. This series captured an emotional and sensitive moment and told a vivid, gripping, and interactive story that was accessible to anyone at any time or place. The portraits of the individuals brought their stories to life and provided a meaningful way for people to understand the loss of so many people with different backgrounds and unique experiences.

From another perspective using the matching stage, we examine the paid-subscription success of *The Wall Street Journal*. Although other media outlets seek to emulate this process, none has reproduced the success that WSJ.com found online. The success of *The Wall Street Journal* online has been attributed to several factors, but a key has been that the organization has identified its target audience and their needs. On Tuesday, December 23, 2003, *The Wall Street Journal* ran a full-page ad to its advertisers:

> The Wall Street Journal Hits a New Record: 2.6 Million Circulation (for The Wall Street Journal and WSJ.com.) It's official: More people now subscribe to The Wall Street Journal than ever before in its 114-year history. The paid circulation of the print and online Journals is over 2.6 million worldwide and, based on the latest Audit Bureau of Circulations Statement, 2.1 million in the U.S. This powerful combination offers advertisers a large, highly affluent business and consumer audience. To mark this significant milestone, we are introducing Total Journal—a new program that allows advertisers to take maximum advantage of The Journal's vital, unrivaled audience. ("A Message to Advertisers," p. D9)

Such a powerful advertising and marketing statement also links the brand to its historical success offline and its new strength when combined by the convergence of print and online for delivery of news and information. The Wall Street Journal Radio Network, with its 44 radio stations stretching from Michigan to Texas, holds even more potential for a convergence of news and information under the brand name.

Aspects of *The Wall Street Journal's* success with its online operations have been observed in numerous studies (Budde, 1998; Steinbock, 2000). Steinbock's analysis of the online subscription model of WSJ.com provided insightful detail of the birth of the electronic version of the brick and mortar establishment. Steinbock chronicled the research and detail that Dow Jones Co., the parent of WSJ on- and offline, took to successfully launch the established business and economic newspaper online.

The Wall Street Journal emerged online in 1996 as *The Wall Street Journal Interactive*, a paid-subscription model. The *Journal* capitalized on its two established brands—*The Journal* and parent company Dow Jones—and used the strategy "we had to deliver value to customers or we wouldn't survive," according to its online publisher Neil Budde (cited in Steinbock, 2000, p. 178). The goal was to exploit brand identity. The company knew its target audience's economic and educational level and had a reputation as the leader in business and economic news. After a brief trial period online, by September 1996, *Journal Interactive* had 30,000 paid subscribers. The company has kept its focus on its brand and growth and suggested the online unit might be profitable by the end of 2004 (Gates, 2002).

REDEFINING AND RESTRUCTURING

The redefining/restructuring stage usually takes place when the innovation is adjusted to meet the needs of the organization. The dot.com bust of 2001 translated to media organizations cutting staff in their online divisions or, in cases such as Dallas-based Belo, the newspaper, TV, and online units were merged and housed in *The Dallas Morning News* building to streamline and reduce costs and duplications. Use of the Internet and computers continued to grow despite the dot.com bust, so organizations adjusted their reaction to the business change. Strategic approaches to handling the dot.com bubble going flat have ranged from bringing operations inhouse, combining services, or eliminating the online version, which Rupert Murdoch chose to do at News Corp. (Moses, 2001).

The State of the News Media 2004 report suggests that there are three economic models used online: subscription based (e.g., WSJ.com); registration, but free content relying on advertising (e.g., Washingtonpost.com); and a mix of paid and free content (e.g., nytimes.com; The State of the News, 2004). A plethora of examples can be used to examine how these approaches are operationalized in the industry. The goal for most media companies is to find the model that is most suitable to their needs and will eventually translate into a profitable enterprise. This is where the redefining/restructuring stage is applicable because an organization makes adjustments to an innovation to find what best suits its needs.

Media outlets nationwide are making adjustments to optimize delivery of content, products, and services across platforms. For example, *The Cleveland Plain Dealer*, Ohio's largest newspaper, has an affiliation with Cleveland.com, a Web site of "everything Cleveland." This affiliation includes links to WKYC-TV, the NBC affiliate in Cleveland and its sister station in Akron, PAX-TV, a radio site link, Sun Newspapers, and a business publication. This allows for cross-promotion and more exposure to the media outlets across the region and state. The interactive potential and archival capabilities for these organizations are enhanced by the affiliation with Cleveland.com.

This redifining/restructuring stage is where multiple adjustments can be made by an organization to tweak an innovation to its best potential. What may start as an online operation that is a cost center for the parent company can evolve into combined resources within and outside of an organization, paid premium content, paid subscription or special promotions. The potential is unlimited.

CLARIFYING

In the clarifying stage for an innovation within an organization, the use becomes widespread, and its importance becomes clearer for all members of the organization. This is where the surge in the focus on convergence has occurred in the media industry. For example, journalists are trained across business units, newspaper photographers and broadcast camera operators become videographers, and new positions (such as multimedia liaisons) are developed. One business strategy used by several media outlets in 2002 was a push for online registration of Web sites; in some instances, a paid/fee hybrid is in place for certain premium content (Sullivan, 2003).

Also at this stage, the elevation of communication technologies into media organizations takes a more functional path. For example, the issue of content management systems comes into play because technology often plays a dual role of enhancing as well as prohibiting certain operations. For years at most media outlets, the attempt to converge was hampered by different computer systems that did not "talk" to each other, as well as software to upload daily material across platforms. Tribune Company was among many organizations focusing on convergence that grappled with the issue of a lack of software to handle newspaper, online, and video copy simultaneously. "An appalling amount of what we do is 'sneakernet,'" David Underhill, Tribune Company's Vice President for Intergroup Development, stated in 2001 (cited in "Media Convergence," 2003). What occurred in the following years was the development of inhouse content management systems such as Tribune Company's Oxygen, Media General's BudgetBank, and McClatchy Co.'s Nando Media (Campbell, 2002), which help organize, manage, store, and distribute content across computer systems and media platforms. All are illustrative of industry leaders proactively seeking methods to enhance their operations in a converged environment. Private vendors also offer content management software systems, but organizations such as those listed earlier have taken convergence to the clarifying stage by developing the software inhouse. This could be viewed as an example of the commitment to make innovations in their organizations work as expeditiously as possible.

ROUTINIZING

Rogers' fifth stage, routinizing, where the innovation becomes a part of regular activities, is still unfolding for media organizations. The industry as a whole continues to deliberate over strategies and best practices to propel media organizations into the future. The debate over the Federal Communications Commission's (FCC) cross-ownership rule, which entails owning broadcast and print outlets in the same market, will contribute to the evolution of this next stage. The FCC approved the rule change in June 2003, but a federal appeals court rejected the decision in June 2004. Discussion on both sides has centered on a rush by corporate owners to purchase more media, potentially shrinking voices in the marketplace of ideas if the cross-ownership rule is eventually enacted. At this point, the routinizing stage could pick up momentum as organizations recalibrate to adapt to an innovation becoming a fixture. The entire process starts again with the next innovation.

Discussion of Rogers' innovation process in organizations is an appropriate segue to Fidler's (1997) arguments on *media-morphosis*. Fidler coined this term in 1990, which is defined as "the transformation of communication media, usually brought about by the complex interplay of perceived needs, competitive and political pressures, and social and technologic innovations" (p. xv). Mediamorphosis expounds on the issue of innovation and the ways technology has transformed communication media. Fidler argued the changes occur simultaneously and promote an examination of the interdependence of all forms of content delivery, including emerging technologies.

The six fundamental principles of mediamorphosis are (a) coevolution and coexistence, (b) metamorphosis, (c) propagation, (d) survival, (e) opportunity and need, and (f) delayed adoption (Fidler, 1997). The principles help contextualize the process by which emerging technologies are transforming traditional media outlets as they adapt to new media. For example, newspapers did not cease to exist because of the Internet, but rather developed on-line versions (coevolution/coexistence) of the offline product. Every media organization did not hop directly on the Internet entrance ramp (metamorphosis), but entered slowly through the use of Internet service providers (ISPs) such as AOL or, eventually, direct access to the Web. The screen design of media-related Web sites (propagation) has a familiarity to the traditional newspaper layout of centerpiece focus and vertical or horizontal headlines to lead the eye to key information. Traditional print and broadcast outlets are adapting (survival) to new technologies for content delivery, products, and services. Newspapers are a good example because they initially used shovelware—shoveling print content online—but later made adjustments (opportunity and need) to develop original content for the Web that is more reflective of an interactive environment. Fidler's final principle of delayed adoption references Paul Saffo's "30-year-rule" for adoption of new ideas (cited in Fidler, 1997). Traditional media companies are aware of the influence of computers and the Internet, as well as wireless and other portable devices, and have added these channels to their distribution process. However, no one knows for sure exactly *why* and *how* people are using the Internet. They can know *when*, through capturing IP addresses and online registration at Web sites, but once the awe of the technology shakes out will the fascination continue?

Fidler's (1997) mediamorphosis process addresses the evolution of media forms, adoption, enterprise, and eventual widespread use of technology. Fidler identified the evolution of spoken, written, and digital language as changes in the human communication process crystallize the salience of innovative technologies and their impact on media. From this perspective, it is inevitable that media organizations would change their approach to disseminating news, information, and entertainment. The media products and services are also altered because of emerging technologies and require enhanced marketing and branding efforts to stand out among the myriad communication media choices.

Whether from the perspective of Rogers' (1995) innovation in organizations or Fidler's (1997) mediamorphosis principles to research on innovation and adoption research methods and theories (Davis, Bagozzi, & Warshaw, 1989; Dupagne, 1999; Lin, 2003; Vishwanath & Goldhaber, 2003), change is change, and it is here to stay in the media industry. Emerging (digital) technologies have pushed us past traditional print and broadcast delivery to cable, Internet, and wireless delivery, and the future channels and devices are yet to come. With all the changes in the industry, efforts take place to manage what are often called *disruptive technologies* in an organization (Frambach, 1993). Innovation management research addresses concerns regarding managing technology within organizations.

INNOVATION MANAGEMENT

Innovation management research focuses on issues that organizations incur when new technology arises. The research has often addressed new products and competition and privileged the adoption of innovations from the individual or consumer perspective (Edler & Meyer-Krahmer, 2001; Frambach, 1993). Innovation is key in a competitive environment in which organizations adopt changes to remain competitive. Therefore, understanding innovation management from the organization's perspective is salient to understanding their adoption of technology (Frambach, 1993; Saksena & Hollifield, 2002).

Rogers' (1995) definition of *innovation* as "an idea, practice, or object that is perceived as new by an individual or other unit of adoption" (p. 11) is a foundation for examining how media organizations look at the Internet as an innovation for the industry. The Internet has been called both a *channel* and a *medium* by some scholars, and the debate continues on whether it is a mass medium. In this book, the Internet is viewed as a mass medium because it not only provides a one-to-many, but one-to-one as well as two-way communication. "Technology has become an important strategic business asset for many markets and firms," stated Frambach (1993, p. 22). This makes it apparent why media organizations could not watch the future of the Internet unfold without participation. The transformation that computer-driven delivery of content brought to the industry is understandable when one considers that organizations in competitive environments are more likely to adopt an innovation to remain competitive even if it is considered a disruptive technology (Frambach, 1993; Silverthorne, 2002; Tidd, 2001). Corporate leaders recognized the need for a technology strategy and developed tools and best practices to incorporate the changes necessary for the environment (Edler & Meyer-Krahmer, 2001).

USES AND GRATIFICATIONS RESEARCH

Discussion of innovation in organizations is incomplete if we fail to address what audiences will make of all the emerging technologies. Corporate media leaders are eager to build "it" whatever "it" is for content, product, and services through different media. The question is, will the audience come?

Uses and gratifications (U&G) research addressing numerous media and technology devices over the decades (Ruggiero, 2000) provides insight into what may or may not happen as communication technologies evolve. What may happen is known, but how and why for users is an unknown variable because it changes constantly. The term *convergence* may be interpreted different ways. However, *Tampa Tribune* publisher Thelen (2002) once stated that, for news organizations to dominate their market, they must "supply news and information whenever, however and wherever customers desire" (p. 16). Print, online, broadcast, wireless, and cable are current channels on which future technologies will build. Although now a primitive technology, the telegraph left a footprint by separating communication and transportation in the 1800s and served as a forbearer of the technologies that followed. Standage's (1998) *The Victorian Internet* painted a picture not only of the uncertainties the telegraph brought to communication, but its social and political implications as well. The same is true of current technological innovations. In the end, the human factor of individual choice determines what technologies are adopted and stay the course and which fall by the wayside.

A summary of research on different technologies over the decades and what has been gleaned from uses and gratifications research provides insight into how the audience perceives use of technology. Early research in uses and gratifications studied a variety of areas, including quiz shows and soap operas, newspaper reading, and TV and political messages (Blumler & McQuail, 1969; Herzog & Bereleson cited in Ruggiero, 2000). These studies primarily focused on gratifications sought rather than those obtained (Rayburn, 1996). Later, Katz, Blumler, and Gurevitch (1974) provided new insight of media use and behavior by studying gratifications both sought *and* obtained. They identified a U&G model that included five elements: (a) the audience actively engages the media; (b) need, gratification, and media choice are determined individually; (c) the media compete with other need-satisfying sources for audience fulfillment; (d) audience members supply sufficient data for needs assessment and evaluation; and (f) audience orientation is best explored according to the individuals being studied. Such an approach opens the door to the possibility of predicting media consumption, which could be useful in today's environment as new technologies evolve.

A look at traditional communication devices provides additional insight into how it might be used. O'Keefe and Sulanowski (1995) used the U&G approach to study gratifications sought from the telephone and behavior patterns for its use. They identified the telephone as a "pervasive information technology" that has progressed to provide more "media-like services" in contemporary society (p. 922). A telephone survey was conducted through random digit dialing for 597 adults in three Wisconsin counties with a response rate of 52%. The gratifications measured were sociability, entertainment, acquisition, and time management. In a factor analysis of the four gratifications areas, the study found that "having a phone on hand for emergencies appears to be a near-universally accepted function of subscribership" (p. 925). They also found gender and age to be the strongest indicator of sociability use for the telephone and less of an influence for entertainment purposes.

The Internet has increasingly attracted mass communication scholars to study use of the new medium. Eighmey and McCord (1998) used the U&G approach to study how audiences experienced Web site use. In 1995, they used 31 participants—all college graduates with an average age of 30, evenly divided by gender, more than 70% of which were experienced users of the Web. The participants used five commercial Web sites and evaluated them on a rating scale. The study found similar types of uses and gratifications for using the Web as with other media, and it discovered new dimensions such as "personal involvement and continuing relationship" as key to Web use (p. 187).

In a broader approach to studying uses of the web, Webster and Lin (2002) examined Web use as mass behavior and focused on a macrolevel analysis of 1,766 Web sites in 1999 using Nielsen/NetRatings, a proprietary database. The researchers specifically addressed exposure to Web sites and "ignored the needs and gratifications that motivate web use, the disparate ways in which people employ web sites, and the meanings they attribute to their encounters" (p. 8). For illustration of audience size, the Lorenz curve was used. In the study, the "curve ascends slowly across the majority of smaller web sites but turns sharply upward as the effect of the most popular sites is added in" (pp. 6–7). The authors suggested that if there were equally large unique audiences, the curve would have been a straight line rising at a 45-degree angle at what is called the *equity line*, and where it bows down from the line would have suggested evidence of concentration.

The U&G research suggests there is a variation in how audiences use media, their motives for use, and what gratification they may obtain. It is clear from the research that audiences are active and select the media devices in which they choose to engage. But discussion of the research surveyed does not suggest one overwhelming motive or gratification sought or obtained. We glean some insight on why people may select a device, but do not know when and if they will return to that device and if for the same reasons. When new devices enter the market, age, gender, education, and socioeconomic status (SES) might influence use, for example, with the telephone. More research might find cell phones resonate in different ways than the traditional phone and the implications of such change. The new technologies are arriving in as little as 2- to 3-year cycles, thus Saffo's 30-year rule for acceptance of new technologies (Fidler, 1997) provides potential for new inquiry on new devices. Many of these new devices will not stay and receive mass acceptance, but in a new media environment with segmented audiences a device may not necessitate mass appeal for use.

NEW MEDIA RESEARCH

The diversity in research by government, marketing, and private organizations provides some insight into how access and use of new media is occurring. The three studies discussed next are a sample of the type of empirical research being used to better understand how and why people use new media such as the Internet, computers, cell phones, PDAs, and satellite. The first study, *A*

Nation Online: How Americans Are Expanding Their Use of the Internet, was conducted by the U.S. Department of Commerce and released in February 2002. In 2003, the second study, *The Simultaneous Media Use Survey*, was conducted by The Media Center at API. The third study, *The Web Habit: An Ethnographic Study of Web Usage*, was conducted in 2004 by John Carey as part of a series for the Online Publishers Association.

A NATION ONLINE

The growth of new information technologies has increased the use of such technologies by the public. This survey found that in 2001, more than 143 million Americans were online—about 54% of the population. The top online activities include about 45% of people using the Internet for e-mail, 36% for product and service information searches, and 33% for news, weathers, and sports searches. This study spanned demographics and geographic areas and provided more insight into the type of people using the Internet and computers. The study found children and teenagers using the Internet more than any group. Of children between the ages 5 and 17, about 90% or 48 million use computers and 75% of 14- to 17-year-olds and 65% of 10- to 13-year-olds use the Internet (U.S. Department of Commerce, 2002).

The key findings from the study were the increase in Internet use regardless of income, education, age, races, ethnicity, or gender:

- Between December 1998 and September 2001, Internet use by individuals in the lowest-income households (less than $15,000 per year) increased at a 25% annual growth rate. Internet use among individuals in the highest-income households ($75,000 per year or more) increased from a higher base but at a much slower 11% annual growth rate.
- Between August 2000 and September 2001, Internet use among Blacks and Hispanics increased at annual rates of 33% and 30%, respectively. Whites and Asian American and Pacific Islanders experienced annual growth rates of approximately 20% during these same periods.

- Between 1998 and 2001, growth in Internet use among people living in rural households was at an average annual rate of 24%, and the percentage of Internet users in rural areas (53%) is now almost even with the national average (54%). (U.S. Department of Commerce, 2002, pp. 1–2)

The infusion of new communication technologies is having an impact on society, and tools such as computers and the Internet are increasingly playing more of a role in the daily routine.

THE SIMULTANEOUS MEDIA USE SURVEY

Technology is prompting a multitasking society, with 70% of media consumers reporting in a 2003 study that they use multiple forms of media simultaneously. The Simultaneous Media Usage Survey (SIMM) released in 2004 provides insight about how people are using technology. The study was conducted online in October 2003, with 13,414 people responding with a +/– 1% margin of error. The Media Center at API partnered with BIGresearch of Ohio to use its proprietary sampling technique for the survey. Some of the key findings revealed that 66.2% of respondents regularly or occasionally watch TV while online; 74.2% regularly or occasionally watch TV and read the newspaper at the same time; and while waiting for downloads from the Internet, 52.1% listen to the radio, 61.8% watch TV, and 20.2% reading the newspaper (Video Briefing, 2004). This research indicates that use of different forms of media is becoming more of a regular occurrence. The choices have increased, and many people are integrating their media choices rather than abandoning one for the other. A recent study on the habits of people using the Web provides insight into some of these choices.

THE WEB HABIT

People use the Web for different reasons and in different ways. Carey (2004) conducted an ethnographic study of the Internet with 44 people in New York, California, Florida, and Massachusetts. Carey grouped his findings from the qualitative research into four areas: (a) how and where users access the Web, (b) the transformation of the Web from a work tool into a routine part of everyday social life, (c) the emergence of Web habits, and (d) Web content usage. According to the study, more and more people are using the Web in all aspects of their lives at work, home, school, coffee shops, airports, and more. For most people, computer and Web use started in the workplace, but their use is increasingly becoming a part of everyday life (Carey, 2004). Habits for using the Web have emerged because of routine uses. Carey found some people have developed a habit of having coffee while checking the Web for online news in the morning. Another example is the use of the Web as a "psychological comfort such as keeping [one] company or occupying time" (p. 12). Carey noted that use of the content on the Web is more than e-mail and instant messaging. Although information and communication are central uses of the web, shopping and entertainment have also become important parts of Web use (Carey, 2004).

The summary of these recent studies on how new technologies are being used indicates that Internet use is becoming more routine and usage varies for individuals. For media organizations and the convergence process, this is insightful because of the need to better understand how and why people use technology. Whether developing content, products, or services, there is a need to know the audience and what they might be looking for in these areas. Rogers' (1995) diffusion of innovations makes it clear that adoption of any new idea or device follows a process that determines whether it will be accepted. Organizations that do not address this concern will find several initiatives unsuccessful. The adoption process in organizations is an internal one that helps to create an understanding of the change within before ideas and devices are taken to the public.

REFERENCES

Blumler, J. G., & McQuail, D. (1969). *Television in politics*. Chicago: University of Chicago Press.

Budde, N. (1998). *The Wall Street Journal*: Blending the old with the new. Institute for Cyberinformation (Online). Accessed March 24, 2003, from http://www.ici.kent.edu

Campbell, M. (2002, January 11). Newspapers have developed new ways to cross media—and now market them to others. *Editor & Publisher, 135*(6), 18–29.

Carey, J. (2004). The web habit: An ethnographic study of web usage. *Online Publishers Association White Paper, 2*(1), 1–24. Retrieved January 31, 2004, from http://www.online-publishers.org.

Carlson, D. (2003). The history of online journalism. In K. Kawamoto (Ed.), *Digital Journalism: Emerging media and the Changing horizons of journalism* (pp. 31–55). Lanham, MD: Rowman & Littlefield.

Davis, F. D., Bagozzi, R. P., & Warshaw, P. R. (1989). User acceptance of Computer technology: A comparison of two theoretical models. *Management Science, 35*(8), 982–1003.

Detroit newspaper rivalry may end soon. (1985, August 25). *The Washington Post,* pp. F1, F3.

Dizard, W. (2000). *Old media new media: Mass communication in the information age.* New York: Longman.

Dupagne, M. (1999). Exploring the characteristics of potential high-definition television adopters. *Journal of Media Economics, 12,* 35–50.

Editor & Publisher International Yearbook, 81st ed. (2001). New York: The Editor & Publisher.

Edler, J., & Meyer-Krahmer, F. (2001). Managing technology in the top-r&d-spending companies worldwide—results of a global survey. *Engineering Management Journal, 13*(1), 5–11.

Eighmey, J., & McCord, L. (1998). Adding value in the information age: Uses and gratifications of sites on the world wide web. *Journal of Business Research, 41,* 187–194.

Fidler, R. (1997). *Mediamorphosis: Understanding new media.* Thousand Oaks, CA: Pine Forge Press.

Frambach, R. T. (1993). An integrated model of organizational adoption and diffusion of innovations. *European Journal of Marketing, 27*(5), 22–41.

Gates, D. (2002, July 10). News sites hustle for profitability. Online Journalism Review. Retrieved July 11, 2002, from http://www.ojr.org/ojr/future/1026348638.php

Gonyea, D., & Hoyt, M. (1997, May/June). Fallout from Detroit: From a brutal strike, bitter lessons and lasting losses. *Columbia Journalism Review* [Online]. Retrieved December 4, 2004, from http://archives.cjr.org

Katz, E., Blumler, J., & Gurevitch, M. (1974). Utilization of mass communication by the individual. In J. Blumler & E. Katz (Eds.), *The uses of mass communication: Current perspectives on gratifications research* (pp. 19–34). Beverly Hills, CA: Sage.

Kawamato, K. (Ed.). (2003). *Digital journalism: Emerging media and the changing horizons of journalism.* Langham, MD: Rowman & Littlefield.

Lin, C. A. (2003). An interactive communication adoption technology model. *Communication Theory, 13*(4), 345–365.

Media convergence faces technical barriers. (2001). [Electronic Version]. *The Quill, 89*(2), 7. Retrieved March 19, 2003, from Infotrac.

A message to advertisers: The Wall Street Journal hits a new record. (2003, December 23). *The Wall Street Journal*, p. D9.

Moses, L. (2001). Finis for fun and games as online layoffs mount. *Editor & Publisher, 134*(3), 5–6.

Multi-channel media brands: Attitudinal and usage study. (2004). Online Publishers Association and Frank N. Magid Associates Inc. [Electronic Version]. Retrieved February 20, 2004, from http://www. onlinepublishers.org

Newspapers hold 7 spots on top 20 news site list. (2004, March 19). *Editor & Publisher* [Electronic Version]. Retrieved March 22, 2004, from http://www.mediainfo.com/eandp/news/article_display.jsp?vnu_content_id=1000466977

O'Keefe, G. J., & Sulanowski, B. K. (1995). More than just talk: Uses, gratifications, and the telephone. *Journalism & Mass Communication Quarterly, 72*(4), 922–933.

Rayburn, J. D. (1996). Uses and gratifications. In M. B. Salwen & D. W. Stacks (Eds.), *An integrated approach to communication theory and research* (pp. 145–163). Mahwah, NJ: Lawrence Erlbaum Associates.

Rogers, E. M. (1995). *Diffusion of innovations* (4th ed.). New York: The Free Press.

Ruggiero, T. E. (2000). Uses and gratifications theory in the 21st century. *Mass Communication & Society, 3*(1), 3–37.

Saksena, S., & Hollifield, C. A. (2002). *Managing innovation: U.S. newspapers and the development of online editions.* Unpublished manuscript.

Silverthorne, S. (2002). Read all about it! Newspapers lose web war. In J. Simon (Ed.), *Re-thinking the web: The media has an ever-changing relationship with the internet* (pp. 18–19). Publication for American Society of Newspaper Editors' Interactive Committee. Tampa, FL: *The Tampa Tribune.*

Standage, T. (1998). *The Victorian internet: The remarkable story of the telegraph and the nineteenth century's on-line pioneers.* New York: Walker & Co.

The state of the news media 2004: An annual report on american journalism. (2004). Project for Excellence in Journalism. Retrieved March 16, 2004, from http://www.Journalism.org

Steinbock, D. (2000). Building dynamic capabilities: The Wall Street Journal interactive edition: A successful online subscription model

(1993–2000). *The International Journal of Media Management, 2*(3), 178–194.

Sullivan, C. (2003, January 20). By thinking the once-unthinkable-web site registration as the norm-newspapers are boosting net revenue. *Editor & Publisher, 136*(3), 11–21.

Thelen, G. (2002). Convergence is coming: Future newsrooms will require specialists who can learn to adapt. *Quill, 90*(6), 16.

Tidd, J. (2001). Innovation management in context: Environment, organization and performance. *International Journal of Management Reviews, 3*(3), 169–183.

Video briefing from BIG research. (2004). The Media Center at the American Press Institute. Retrieved April 7, 2004, from http://mediacenter.org/mediamorphosis/bigresearch

U.S. Department of Commerce. (2002). *A nation online: How americans are expanding their use of the internet.* Washington, DC: Author.

Vishwanath, A., & Goldhaber, G. M. (2003). An examination of factors contributing to adoption decisions among late-diffused technology products. *New Media & Society, 5*(4), 547–572.

Webster, J. G., & Lin, S. (2002). The internet audience: Web use as mass behavior. *Journal of Broadcasting & Electronic Media, 46*(1), 1–12.

II

Convergence in Action

4

Tribune Company: A Convergence Pioneer Since the 1900s

Clarence Darrow and the Scopes Monkey Trial may be hidden in the recesses of legal and social history, but accounts of media history during that period should include coverage of the trial by the *Chicago Tribune* and its sister radio station, WGN. The call letters WGN stand for "World's Greatest Newspaper," and that is exactly what the *Tribune*, or the late Colonel Robert McCormick, wanted the public to think whenever reading its pages in the heady days of the 1920s. Fast forward to the 21st century, and you might wonder what this has to do with convergence—everything when it comes to Tribune Company. The cross-promotion of the radio station and newspaper across the two mediums in the 1920s was an early form of convergence nearly 70 years before it was the phenomena that traverses through media organizations seeking to integrate the potential and promise of technology into their operations. The significance of WGN is apparent in the "About Tribune History" link on the corporate Web site.

> Chicago's WGN Radio (720 AM) went on the air in 1924, its call letters reflecting the *Chicago Tribune's* renowned slogan, "World's Greatest Newspaper." The station was an innovator from the start. It was first to broadcast the World Series, the Indianapolis 500 and the Kentucky Derby, and broke new ground by introducing microphones in the courtroom during the famous 1925 Scopes "monkey trial" in

Tennessee. Today, Tribune's original broadcast property is a 50,000-watt Midwest powerhouse. (Tribune.com, 2004, par. 5)

Chicago Tribune Senior Vice President and Executive Editor, Ann Marie Lipinski, stated that an old *Tribune* photograph of the Scopes Trial with a lone picture of a WGN radio microphone is one of her favorite pictures and a testament to Colonel McCormick as a "great technological visionary" (Lipinski, 2000, p. 9) (see Fig. 4.1). What might have appeared as excessive newspaper publicity in those days was really interesting foresight into what Tribune Company has come to symbolize in the age of convergence. Tribune Tower sits as a beacon on Michigan Avenue towering over the nearby Chicago River with its plethora of drawbridges threaded along the river. The Tower is more than a landmark—it is home to a 158-year-old media tradition that includes newspapers, TV, radio, and cable Superstation WGN. The Chicago Cubs Major League Baseball team provides a bounty of programming, with 70 games aired each year ("Swinging," 2004). Superstation WGN celebrated its 25th anniversary in 2004. Table 4.1 highlights significant aspects of Superstation WGN.

TRADITIONAL CONVERGENCE PIONEER

Chicago-based Tribune Company is a traditional convergence pioneer dating to the early 1900s. It is traditional in the sense that the *Chicago Tribune* newspaper is a historical print icon that capitalized on its "synergies" with WGN radio before such terms as *synergy* and *convergence* were the well-known vernacular in the industry. Tribune was chosen for this case study based on its tradition of utilizing all of its business units to cross-promote and support efforts to get the brand before the public. It is a laboratory for convergence because it blends its business units in Chicago in strategic ways that take advantage of its position of cross-ownership of media in a major market. The analytical approach for the three case studies in Part II of this book is explanation building—an inductive approach that uses the collected data to build an explanation about the case (Haas, 2000). Tribune employees quoted in this

FIG. 4.1.   This undated photo illustrates a broadcast session at WGN
Radio. Photo courtesy of Tribune Company.

TABLE 4.1

Superstation WGN at 25

Superstation WGN: 25 years of programming, 1979–2004
- 100% analog distribution
- 50 to 60 million viewers
- 70 Chicago Cubs games aired each year
- 700-title movie library
- First original programming to debut in 2005
- Local counterpart WGN-TV Chicago

Source. Superstation WGN 25th anniversary. (2004, April 5). Broadcasting & Cable 134 (14).

chapter were interviewed at different intervals starting in 2002 and 2004. This case study explicates specific elements of Tribune operations in Chicago to illustrate present-day efforts to move convergence forward by utilizing the resources across business units.

First, it most be noted that Tribune Company was grandfathered into the 1975 Federal Communications Commission (FCC) cross-ownership act because it owned its properties before the rule was enacted. Therefore, the company has been rewarded by the opportunity to own a number of successful media properties in the same market. The FCC attempts in 2003 to lift the cross-ownership ban were halted the following year by a federal court in Philadelphia. Tribune's efforts to capitalize on cross-ownership of properties in the company's other markets have been limited because of the ruling. Therefore, this case study centers on the company's Chicago operations where cross-ownership of media properties has flourished.

Tribune Company's business units in the city include the *Chicago Tribune,* WGN radio and TV, CLTV regional cable, chicagotribune.com, Metromix.com, and the Chicago Cubs. The office of Intergroup Development is handled out of Chicago, and Tribune Interactive incorporates all of the Web sites for Tribune. Other media holdings are discussed later, but of note is Tribune's presence in the top three media markets, now owning Times Mir-

ror's the *Los Angles Times* and *New York Newsday* and the oblig-
atory broadcast and electronic holdings in those markets. The
corporate parent's reach extends across print, broadcast, cable,
and the Internet. Table 4.2 contains a list of Tribune Company's
holdings compiled from corporate Web sites and *Columbia Journalism Review's* "Who Owns What" (Columbia, 2004; Tri-
bune.com, 2004).

TABLE 4.2
Tribune Company

Newspapers

> Chicago Tribune, Newsday (Long Island, NY), Los Angeles
> Times, Baltimore Sun, South Florida Sun-Sentinel, Orlando
> Sentinel, The Hartford Courant, The Morning Call (Allentown,
> PA), Daily Press (Hampton Roads, VA), The Advocate (Stamford,
> CT), Greenwich Time (CT), La Opinion (Los Angeles), Exito
> (Chicago), Hoy (New York), El Sentinel (Orlando)

Broadcast

> WGN - Chicago, WPIX - New York, KTLA - Los Angeles, WPHL -
> Philadelphia, WLVI – Boston, KDAF - Dallas, WATL - Atlanta,
> KHWB - Houston, KCPQ - Seattle, KTWB - Seattle, WBZL - Mi-
> ami - Ft. Lauderdale, KWGN - Denver, KTXL - Sacramento,
> WXIN - Indianapolis, WTTV - Indianapolis, KSWB - San Diego,
> WTIC - Hartford/New Haven, WTXX- Hartford, WXMI - Grand
> Rapids, WGNO - New Orleans, WNOL - New Orleans, WPMT -
> Harrisburg, WBDC - Washington, WEWB - Albany, KPLR - St.
> Louis, KWBP - Portland, WB Network, Tribune Entertainment

Cable

> WGN, Chicago Land Television (CLTV), Central Florida News 13

Radio

> WGN–AM (Chicago)

Other

> Chicago Cubs, Tribune Media Services, Classified Ventures (par-
> tial), Brass Ring, Zap 2 It, BlackVoices.com, Chicago magazine,
> CareerBuilders.com, Apartments.com, Cars.com, New Home
> Network, Homespace.com, Calendarlive.com, Metromix.com,
> SouthFlorida.com, 7Cities.com, HRtickets.com,
> ChicagoSports.com, Go2orlando.com

CONVERGENCE IN THE NEWSROOM 1993

A modern-day version of convergence arrived at Tribune in 1993: CLTV, the Chicago area's first and only 24-hour all-news cable channel, aired its first broadcast. The *Chicago Tribune*'s sister station, CLTV, quickly became a model for multimedia content sharing and cross-promotion throughout Tribune Company. Today, Tribune newspapers aggressively partner with the news operations of Tribune TV stations in their markets or with non-Tribune broadcasters, including local radio stations (Tribune.com, 2004, par. 17).

The photo (Fig. 4.2) illustrates the author's entry into the convergence world at the *Chicago Tribune* in 1993, when a converged newsroom opened in one of its news bureaus. The DuPage County newspaper bureau was relocated from Hinsdale to Oak Brook, Illinois, to share facilities with the staff of the new CLTV cable station and an advertising staff for the county. As an assistant bureau chief, the author worked with the bureau chief to acclimate print reporters to an organizational cultural change that included cooperation with the newspaper's sister broadcaster. A half-circle news desk separated the cable operations from the newspaper bureau. The expectation, however, was that resources and facilities would be shared. Print reporters were expected to collaborate on news coverage with the cable journalists in the background on stories, on-camera interviews, and so on. This did not sit well with many of the print journalists who were indoctrinated with the philosophy that they provided the most in-depth coverage through the printed word. Broadcasters were believed to be visual and offer snippets of information to meet 30-second sound bites or limited airtime. Such notions still exist, but have evolved over the years, and many print journalists in Chicago comfortably collaborate and have adapted to the fusion of print, broadcast, and the Internet.

STRUCTURE OF CHICAGO OPERATIONS

The convergence structure in Chicago is detailed in an internal document describing multimedia journalism operations. This document details the organization of units that led to the process of

FIG. 4.2. The author (center), Jill Rosengard, CLTV assignment
editor, and Michael Adams, director of news and programming, in
the joint CLTV and Chicago Tribune Oak Brook bureau in 1993.
Photo courtesy of Tribune Company.

convergence. Inside Tribune Tower, a TV platform was set up in the
fourth-floor newsroom, and seven other locations throughout the
tower were wired for live camera and studio equipment. Other outlets included a radio booth, Intergroup Operations for broadcasters, and chicagotribune.com. Properties on the lower level of the
Tower are Metromix.com, Blackvoices.com, and Sports.com, and
offsite in a western suburb bureau office is CLTV cable.

Daily, breaking, and suburban news is covered across platforms
and often cross-promoted. In one example of broadcast to Internet

flow, WGN-TV meteorologist, Tom Skilling, prepares information for the weather page for the *Chicago Tribune* and provides a column answering questions posed by the audience. For special projects and investigation, WGN-TV shares content with the newspaper, WGN radio, CLTV, and chicagotribune.com. In addition, audio from WGN radio can be linked to Internet sites. ChicagoSports.com takes sports coverage online and interactive and enhances the traditional coverage in the newspaper's Sports section. The online site includes critics, commentaries, and special projects such as quizzes that increase interactivity. Sports columnists also tape shows for CLTV cable. The Features department at the newspaper has capitalized on the convergence process in numerous ways. Columnists regularly appear on WGN. Movie, theater, and TV reviews are regular features for CLTV cable and WGN. The newspaper reviewers step up their coverage by integrating broadcast and interactive components to newspaper coverage, such as coupling a music review with video and concert clips to appear on Tribune broadcast outlets. The audience has a dynamic experience that allows entry at any point to the content.

The business coverage is lifted from the pages when newspaper columnists appear on a weekly CLTV business show, such as Jobs columnist Carol Kleiman providing career-coaching advice in print and broadcast. A daily business analysis is provided by a newspaper reporter on CLTV. The flow of content from Internet to broadcast and print has an extra with Metromix.com, the entertainment site for the metropolitan Chicago area that started in 1997. The award-winning site is targeted to the 18- to 35-year-old demographic looking for the latest trends, where to go, and what to do in the Chicago area. Metromix.com has continued to build its relationship with the audience, creating forums for interactivity by posting critiques from the audience. Extensions of the brand include Metromix Minute, which previews the latest happening on the WGN morning and noon news. There is now a Metromix the TV Show on CLTV cable that cross-promotes with the Web site and extends the brand even more. Blackvoices.com, a Web site devoted to African-American issues and interests, also has a segment on

CLTV. Reports from chicagotribune.com are also provided weekday mornings on WGN radio.

One example of information flow is a member of the Electronic News group participating in the daily 8:30 a.m. telephone conference call at which representatives are present from *Chicago Tribune*, WGN-TV, WGN-AM, chicagotribune.com, and CLTV. Information gleaned from the conference call can be fed into the newspaper's morning budget meeting as well as the afternoon editorial page one meeting. As a result, at any point during the day, the various units have the opportunity to expand their content to include aspects from another business unit. Content can flow from the *Chicago Tribune*, WGN, the Spanish language newspaper, Exito!, CLTV cable, and Internet sites. The rules for engagement in the process of convergence are discussed in an internal document entitled *Tribune Content Sharing* document. *Content Sharing* sets as one of its goals sharing resources

> to provide the most compelling journalism to our readers and viewers regardless of how they receive it. This is a major cultural shift for all of us. It will require that we all actively pursue ways to share what we know as quickly as possible among the newspaper, television and radio stations and the Internet.... We must all believe that by sharing our resources we are building a stronger and more valuable relationship with our audiences. (Tribune Content, n.d., p. 1)

Mark Hinojosa, associate managing editor for Electronic News, leads the group that focuses on bringing convergence of content online in Chicago. The work of broadcast and online staff intersects by working with WGN, CLTV, and the newspaper. Hinojosa views their model of operations as producing professional TV on TV just as the newspaper is produced at a certain level that has a national reputation. However, when efforts are made to move to online presentation, Hinojosa suggested, "We want to produce at a level that when we converge or when we use our content, we want to put it out at a level that to the viewer it's seamless" (personal communication, July 8, 2002). The goal is for the distribution platform to become invisible. The content is distributed without losing the quality. Hinojosa wants the audience to be satisfied whether they see the content on TV, read it in the newspaper, hear it on the radio, or access it on the Internet.

According to Mitchell Locin, senior editor for Electronic News, the rules of engagement in the *Content Sharing* document sets guidelines for integrating convergence into daily performance operations. "The cultural shift in the organization is to think of multimedia" (M. Locin, personal communication, July 8, 2002). The war metaphor, *rules of engagement*, is used to specifically address how resources and content will be shared and cross-promoted. For example, permission to use content across platforms is not taken for granted. The process includes notifying the originating desk before using content in a separate unit. Content-sharing managers or editors are in place to facilitate the process of sharing content across platforms. In addition to Tribune Company, other media organizations use this term to describe the pact for internal processes to define how convergence will work across business units. Some of the key areas of emphasis are flexibility, change, content sharing, and multiplatforms. The Interactive group includes chicagotribune.com, breaking news, Shared News Service, and Electronic News group digitizing broadcast packages for the Web feed room.

INTEGRATED OPERATIONS

Journalists, editors, and managers at the operations in Chicago have various takes on what convergence means at their organization. This book focuses on convergence as a concept and process. Using a series of in-depth interviews and participant observation in 2002 and 2004 of Tribune employees and operations in Chicago reveals numerous perspectives on how the process impacts organizational culture, individuals, business units, and the corporate parent company. Whereas convergence or cross-platform delivery is welcome or tolerated by some, others still find the complexities of convergence, its implications, and long-term impact as unsettled territory.

Allan Johnson is a TV writer for the *Chicago Tribune* who has found a niche in using the print and broadcast outlets to distribute his work. Johnson characterized the convergence operations in Chicago as a "storyteller getting the opportunity to tell your story in different media" (A. Johnson, personal interview, July 9, 2002). He suggested there are several components to working across platforms, one of which he views as "thinking visually." Johnson knows what he will cover in his newspaper articles and tries to envision ways to incorporate those efforts into broadcast coverage.

Johnson used as an example of convergence his work on the 2002 Emmy nominations. As Johnson prepared for print coverage, he considered how he might incorporate a broadcast component. He views the process as using "different muscles" to get at a story in a different way.

> I just write a different script which talks about the same thing that I'm talking about in the newspaper, but I'll use different phrases. I can go in different directions. And that's been great. I mean a lot of reporters—I think a lot more now than there was before—but a lot or reporters, you know, just don't get with that. The only thing they think about is doing newspaper. (A. Johnson, personal interview, July 9, 2002)

There is also the issue of increased exposure that Johnson feels his work will get when distributed across mediums. Johnson says as a journalist he is a storyteller, and the integration of media allows the story to be told in different venues. Johnson notes that there is no additional pay for applying multimedia uses for work, and that is problematic for most journalists. He has adopted an approach of seizing the opportunity for more exposure of his work as this process evolves in the organization. "If you are a storyteller, if that's what you like, if you like writing stories, and telling stories, and crafting stories, you've got another way to do it. That's how you have to do it. You can't worry about the money" (A. Johnson, personal communication, July 9, 2002).

However, many employees are concerned about additional compensation for additional work and the direction of an organization.

"You know, you realize that this is what the company wants to do. It's not going to stop. It's where they are at, and that's where you need to be" (A. Johnson, personal interview, July 9, 2002). Johnson's feedback on his work is channeled through several outlets, including e-mail, CLTV cable, and WGN radio, where he gets interaction with readers and viewers on different levels. An e-mail may be prompted by someone hearing Johnson on WGN radio or seeing him on CLTV cable. In Johnson's view, people are paying attention, and there is an opportunity to make use of the channels.

Although Johnson offers a microlevel, individual perspective on convergence, there is a macro, organizational level to be addressed. During an interview in 2002, David Underhill, vice president for Intergroup Development at Tribune Company, was quick to clarify that convergence is not a buzzword or something new to Tribune considering WGN radio and the launching of CLTV cable in 1993. These two units are examples of a continuum for Tribune in adapting to changes in the media industry. A historical timeline on the corporate Web site reflects Tribune's active movement in acquiring new and diversified media properties since the *Chicago Tribune* newspaper first published in 1847 (Tribune.com, 2004). Underhill contended that by sharing resources the company is able to "create new values" across Tribune properties (D. Underhill, personal interview, July 9, 2002).

According to Underhill, Tribune has been active in the area of convergence, noting the 10-year anniversary of CLTV in 2003, but the story is a century old when you include WGN radio's launch in 1924.

> Arguably that's the start of convergence, but during most of those time frames, up until the last 10 years, or so, we didn't encourage these different businesses to work together. We encouraged them, in many respects, not to. The culture was "stay separate." The culture was "compete," and the last 10 years in electronic media, in general, have changed the definition of competition. Somebody said real competition for all media is the clock. (D. Underhill, personal communication, July 9, 2002)

On the clock are 24 hours daily to accomplish whatever goals the company sets for content and distribution. The content, product, or service must be gathered, assembled, and distributed within the daily time frame. In that distribution process, which platforms suits what content must be adjusted and adapted.

Underhill asserted that, from an organizational perspective, convergence is a business question that centers on how to integrate operations across units.

> The concept of value from convergence is a concept of value in many different ways. It can be journalistic value. It can be better coverage, broader coverage, more deep, more rich. You know journalistic value is certainly a prime driver. It can also be a pure economic value, if you sell more advertising, if you have cross-media advertising as Tribune does, we have teams of people who sell across multiple platforms. (D. Underhill, personal communication, July 9, 2002)

The value opportunities are what the organization can focus on for development. For example, a challenge for the newspaper industry is the decline in readership in the 18- to 30-year-old bracket. Underhill stated that Tribune sees this as a logical opportunity for its electronic media strategy to support this market. From the online Web sites to Tribune's WB network-affiliated stations, the company can be "strategic of how we extend our journalism to the audiences that those television stations are really, really going to get it, we will be strategically successful with 18 to 34s" (D. Underhill, personal communication, July 9, 2002). Underhill added that the goal from the journalistic side is to keep the core enterprise strong so that whatever is delivered to the door, through the Internet, by TV, radio, or satellite a hundred years from now, is the "*Chicago Tribune*, and the *LA Times*, and the *Baltimore Sun*" (D. Underhill, personal communication, July 9, 2002).

Although this chapter case study is focused on Tribune's Chicago operations, Underhill cited one of the company's operations in Connecticut as another way to examine the subject. The *Hartford Courant* and the company's TV station WTIC-TV have accomplished a great deal in convergence over a short period of time. The Web site CTmail.com, a statewide Web site, is part of the cross-promoting. At the *Courant*, Ellen Burns, a former TV professional, was hired to gather and package newspaper content for TV and cable. Underhill stated that, although it is a smaller market than Chicago, about a 27 or 28 designated market area range, evidence can be seen of the success of integration.

By 2004, David Underhill was president and CEO of Tribune's CLTV Chicagoland Television. Underhill saw the convergence process moving forward in ways that continue to benefit the organization. The connectivity occurs from the daily conference calls with the other business units to complimentary news cycles for the platforms being used to release content. Underhill said the organization's culture is changing "one by one, and case by case" (personal communication, November 10, 2004). According to Underhill, CLTV reach is beyond the western suburbs, where the station is located, and incorporates some of the city of Chicago, which continues to extend the Tribune brand. He finds CLTV uniquely different from the newspaper with huge brand equity, large audience metrics, reaching different people. The platforms can compliment each other while taking advantage of improved technology, flexibility of a virtual newsroom, and increases in broadband connectivity. Underhill believes the biggest competition for the company is the "clock—time." From a convergence perspective, "Content, core knowledge, and storytelling are platform specific; platform agnostic is the story" (D. Underhill, personal communication, November 10, 2004).

In Chicago, it appears what an individual brings to a converged operation helps to shape his or her perspective. Tom Garritano, a former video producer who joined the Tribune's multimedia group, is often found in the second-floor studio editing room. Garritano wears many hats and uses the sports metaphor of *utility player* to describe his role (T. Garritano, personal communication, July 10, 2002). He communicates with the broadcast, newspaper, and online operations to exchange information. From an editorial conference call, he transcribes and updates the different parties on what each unit is planning. If decisions are made to create a broadcast component to a print or online story, Garritano can help facilitate the process.

Garritano acknowledges that the Web is a conduit for cross-promotions as well as other packages that can be created. For example, if chicagotribune.com seeks video to support a breaking news story, he can be contacted to facilitate that process. According to Garritano, a system is in place that takes only 5 minutes to encode and place video into a server where it can be accessed by the online operations. The company's profile server is a vehicle that helps move this process across platforms. If WGN or CLTV calls to say, "Can you give us this raw video or can you give us this edited package. Can you put it, either feed it to us or put it, in the profile server. That's another example of shared use of how everybody has access to it. Our broadcast partners and us have access to the server where we can store video and retrieve video, just one central server" (T. Garritano, personal communication, July 10, 2002). The profile server is part of the continuous effort to make content available to all Tribune properties for use where it is best suited, according to Garritano.

Expanding the reach of content is what Ben Estes, editor of ChicagoTribune.com, and his staff work daily to make happen. Estes has watched the ebb and flow of the online operations. In an interview in 2002, he talked about how the Internet offers the opportunity for instant information, but the convergence process includes planning for the proper release of that information. In the past, "Some pieces of information (were released) earlier than somebody may have wanted.... And we have had some cases where you just couldn't have arranged it any better" (B. Estes, personal communication, July 10, 2002). For Estes it is essential for convergence that decisions are made on what content goes on which platform or the best method for conveying and releasing information.

The concept of convergence may be understood internally, but Tribune, like other companies, needs to find ways for the public to understand exactly what convergence means to them. Estes added, "We've tried variations on this, but we really haven't come up with the method to put value to all of this.... We are still kind of in the middle of it now" (personal communication, July 10, 2002). Estes suggested identifying hard costs for marketing the platforms to the public and establishing value is illusive; the newspaper runs TV spots on WGN, but how does the company document gain based on cross-promotion?

"What's the value benefit to every night having tomorrow's headlines tonight on the WGN news? I mean the nine o'clock news? It comes on every night, it's there, it's usually on the same time, people expect it; it's promoted. So how many people then look at that and turn around and buy the paper?" (B. Estes, personal communication, July 10, 2002). These are tough questions that Tribune needs to find substantive answers. "It's those kinds of things that we really had to put a hard number on. So when we go out in the world, we can point out all these different things that we're doing." Tribune brand is well known in the market and it has presence, but the benefits of convergence are not concrete for the public.

Estes said convergence is unclear to some because they know Tribune's history as a producer of newspaper, TV, and radio content, but the history of online operations is still relatively young. Convergence practices do not have the history of newspapers and broadcast. Other concerns in addition to marketing and advertising are readership for newspapers and if the other platforms and cross-promotion help drive audiences across print, broadcast, and online. Estes cited an example of one of the newspaper's sports writers who has covered high school sports for years and has recognition and credibility. The writer's use of another platform—online or broadcast—gives him more reach. However, Tribune and other media must find ways to capture the cross use of platforms and quantify the use in a manner that is understandable to those inside and outside the media.

Another component of convergence in Chicago is the Metromix.com Web site. Metromix.com has settled into its niche in ways that have resulted in internal and external recognition of the site. In May 2004, Metromix editor, Leigh Behrens, accepted the Digital Edge Award from the Newspaper Association of America. Metromix.com was awarded Best Entertainment Site and recognized for focusing on "useful, relevant, and credible content" that has created the right formula for its audience.

During an interview in 2002, Behrens stated the site has continued to build a relationship with its audience that is capturing the type of information they seek. "What we really try to do is serve a local audience with great entertainment choices, and every day we do try to deliver a sense of the best things to do in the city" (L. Behrens, personal communication, July 8, 2002). For Metromix, there is an immediacy the site tries to provide for the audience by giving them useful content. "We've taken advantage of what we've tried to learn along the way about what our audience wants and what it needs and they tell us over and over again it is utility" (L. Behrens, personal communication, July 8, 2002).

Such utility includes movie and concert reviews. Behrens pointed out that special dining sections from a database of some 9,000 restaurants keeps the audience abreast of when, where, and what to eat. There are interactive reviews by readers that Metromix uses to get a perspective and reaction from the audience. Those reviews include a group of "Margarita Girls" touring town for the best spots to have a margarita or the "Beer Garden Guys" traversing the metropolitan area for the best beer gardens. These are users of the Web site who volunteered to participate in the interactive reviewing, providing that utility of content on the site that Behrens identified as important to her audience. According to Behrens, the idea is to stay current and relevant on Metromix. It is an eclectic place that connects by keeping a pulse on change and trying to catch the trends. The convergence process is accentuated due to content sharing with the *Friday* section of the newspaper, or CLTV and Metromix the TV Show, or WGN and the Internet site. Chicago is a tourism mecca, and entertainment is a powerful draw to the city and Web site. Behrens suggested that anyone who wants to be involved with convergence efforts needs to think about the audience and different ways to deliver content to that audience—being creative, thinking outside of the box with journalistic values entrenched, and knowing what is news, how to write, when to write, and good grammar. Behrens considers all those ingredients key to someone being a part of the Metromix staff.

The connection to audience for Metromix continues to improve. Behrens has three mailboxes that are inundated with feedback and suggestions. Behrens and her staff seek to make sense of what they learn and find new ways to present the content. The recognition by the national award is one metric of knowing that Metromix connected, but in the long-term it will be relationships with audience, creating revenue, and staying relevant.

> That's exactly what we are looking for to really build this relationship with our audience and it's really been astounding in many ways to see the relationship that we have created so all of your producers also answer their own mail. We're responding from people locally and from far places all over Europe who say, "I heard of Metromix and what are the things that I should be doing in Chicago?" (L. Behrens, personal communication, July 8, 2002)

Behrens' background is on the newspaper side, and she knows the power of brand and reach and is using the online vehicle to continue that push toward the audience and its needs in an electronic environment.

For James Warren, Deputy Manager Editor/Features at the *Chicago Tribune*, convergence is an extension of his experience at the company. A former reporter and Washington Bureau chief, Warren is often seen on the Sunday morning news shows out of Washington. Warren's experience in the Washington bureau where Tribune Company has converged resources from its Chicago, Los Angeles, and New York media provides insight into cultural changes when different platforms integrate resources and content.

> When I say cultural, I sort of mean the mutual suspicions that are there particularly with the war of tradition (newspapers) with members of broadcasting from one standpoint or another. But mutual suspicions sort of died off in time as they realized—came to understand more about the way the other guy operated. (J. Warren, personal communication, July 12, 2002)

Warren suggested there are still tensions from diehards on both print and broadcast in adapting to convergence. For example, it is not an easy process for a print journalist to conduct a live, on-air interview, but over time several *Tribune* journalists are making the transition.

> I think you probably make the case partly by arguing that in the long term there are substantial benefits and efficiency and quality that can be had by changing the cultures. And if you look at it in a short-term perspective, you're not going to see any benefits. That's the bottom line. But, maybe 10 or 20 years down the pike, if you look at your TV stations and newspapers have gained advertising or gained circulation or viewership as a result of these cooperative ventures, then we can say, yes, see this thing worked. (J. Warren, personal communication, July 12, 2002)

According to Warren, the benefits to TV or newspaper consumers must be explored when considering convergence. A case needs to be made for shareholder benefit and what the process brings to the company. It becomes problematic if convergence is a code word for downsizing and a company faces the risk of diluting the product or losing audience.

Choices are important to the audience when using a company's technology. Columnist James Coates writes the Binary Beat column on technology for the *Chicago Tribune* and examines uses of new technology from software to hardware and within organizations and by individuals. Coates' technology column is also uploaded to the Web site. In that capacity, hypertext links allow the audience to move outside of Coates' work to areas to which he points them for further information. "So when you took my column off the printed page and put it on the computer and there's hot links, there is a little value added" (J. Coates, personal communication, July 12, 2002). However, Coates suggested that the economics of the Web site in the post-2001 dot.com bust does not dictate big projects being developed for the Web. Tribune and other companies lost money on early online operations and staffs are smaller now, so convergence must be conducted within the realm of resources and what attracts the audience (Moses, 2001; Lindemann, 2001).

Coates suggested that the awe and wonder of computers, the Internet, and the technology to create different distribution approaches is settling down to a routine of what works. The culture has changed and some things are working, but Coates does not detect any big changes on the front. "You know, we're still thinking that our lives are going to be in complete flux because we are going to have to go on the air. We're going to have to be on TV. We're not TV people at all. And, so they don't really put us on the air too much" (J. Coates, personal communication, July 12, 2002).

Coates contended that convergence efforts appear to be working well in Chicago, but he does not see any revolutionary changes because the types of content the company would offer requires broadband, which is not widely used in homes. If, in the future, you go to a Chicago Web site and a window pops up for CLTV, it will require broadband to take full advantage of the video. The public is not signing up in large numbers to add the service at home. Most people are still accessing the Web during the day at work with T1 lines and broadband. When they are home, the connections slow down to 56K dial-up, and many people are content with this method. Coates' plan for extending the technology would include setting up the framework for the public:

> If I were president of the United States, I would spend all of the money I possibly could on putting out broadband connection in everybody's home. I'd do it as a welfare project. I'd just do it. Everybody's house there would be a little government box on the side of the house, and it would be broadband.... It would be a DHCP (dynamic host configuration protocol), which is the protocol. That anybody, when you have a DHCP network, anybody can just go to the computer room, and the computer just goes online. It is just magic. (J. Coates, personal communication, July 12, 2002)

Coates contended that if you get the broadband to people's houses, then you can expand the type of content provided. He noted, however, that it is currently too expensive and people do not want it. During a 2002 interview, Coates stated that most people are operating with their basic dial-up. Broadband is another utility and another item to pay for in the household. This is a challenge for

Tribune and other media companies that develop different types of content that expand the types of technology people need to take advantage of the product. Coates cited as an example of the slow technology change Tribune Company's use of data from WGN broadcasts using band left over from their broadcasts. A person in a Chicago house would buy a box to watch WGN and get on the Internet. There were links to click on headlines, news stories, recipes, and sports scores. The company put a lot of money time and energy into the project, but it did not work because the public did not catch on. Coates predicted that it could be 10 years (2012 or later) before the industry starts to settle down to what technology will work and be used internally and externally by the audience.

CONVERGENCE IN ACTION

An example of cross-promotion in Chicago is evident in *Chicago Tribune* movie critic Mike Wilmington's show, "Movie Mix," which he tapes for CLTV. The broadcast reviews are connected to Wilmington's newspaper columns and reviews, which also appear on Metromix.com. The movie reviews run Friday nights on TV. John Owens, a news editor for Electronic News, edits Wilmington tapes using Discreet, a computer-based nonlinear editing system. Once the tape is edited, it is ready for distribution on Tribune broadcast platforms.

The author observed the inhouse video process, joining Brad Piper, senior video producer, and Eric Scott, executive producer, to tape a critic package with Rick Morrissey, baseball writer for the *Chicago Tribune*. Morrissey was in the studio after covering the 2002 All-Star Game in Milwaukee. During the game, Major League Baseball Commissioner Bud Selig made a controversial call in the 11th inning when the teams were tied and both had run out of pitchers. Morrissey wrote a story for the newspaper and was using the broadcast taping to provide further emphasis. Critics write their own broadcast scripts, but because Morrissey was returning from the road, the script was written by Scott.

The taping took place in a studio on the second floor of Tribune Tower. The producers use a key wall of a plain blue background so that images can be added later. A disk of the script is inserted in the computer connected to the camera teleprompter. As Morrissey practiced the script, Piper set up the lights, sound, and camera. The segment was taped, and in about 30 minutes Morrissey's role in the process was complete. Piper edited the tape and placed it on the Profile Server, which enabled CLTV to grab the spot for broadcast later in the week. Tribune's advantage is having inhouse production capabilities that allow print journalists to work with broadcast to produce electronic material. Morrissey's action increases the exposure to his work across print, broadcast, and online, and the company integrates the components for maximum reach to the audience.

Morrissey's taping illustrates Tribune's efforts to make the convergence process a norm in the organization. The receptiveness on the part of all parties, such as the Morrissey taping, allows the process to move forward and create a flow of content. The possibilities are endless in creating arrangements that provide multiple outlets for content generated in one unit for distribution on other platforms.

BUSINESS AND ECONOMICS

Tribune executives, as well as leaders at other media companies, are vague when it comes to discussing revenue from online operations or cross-sales and promotions for business units. In the 1990s, several companies rushed to start online units as separate business components that were often cost centers. They were line items in budgets to provide staff and resources, but were not generating income. By the dot.com bust of 2001, several media companies had reduced their online staffs and brought them inhouse. The amounts lost are suggested in the millions, but definitive figures are not clear. Today, Tribune and media executives at other companies speak of incremental advertising, cross-sales and promotions programs, and ad revenues in their Interactive operations increasing.

The financial wherewithal of Tribune Company supports its commitment to convergence. Corporate resources are used to accelerate the progress of various business units. Annual reports and Form 10-Ks from 2001 to 2003 reveal steady progress at the media giant and its diversified properties. The 2001 Annual Report: *Journalism at its Best* revealed that 2001 revenues were $5.3 billion. At that time, the company owned 23 TV stations and one cable station; programming included Tribune Entertainment and Chicago Cubs. In addition, there were 11 newspapers, 4 Hispanic market newspapers, Tribune Media Services syndication, and CLTV cable programming in Chicago, and Tribune Interactive operated more than 50 Web sites, with a combined 7 million unique visitors a month.

According to John Madigan, Tribune chairman and CEO, "Great journalism has always been Tribune Company's foundation. Our success depends on it. In 2001, we were reminded how much the American people depend on it, too" (Tribune Company, 2001, p. 1). The annual report introduction details the company's coverage of the 9/11 tragedy across print, broadcast, and online. "The value of Tribune's multimedia strategy was affirmed as our print, broadcast and online news teams worked together to deliver news and information when people needed it most" (p. 2). Despite the national tragedy and the economic conditions that year, the company generated $1.24 billion in operation cash. Cost containment was one of the reasons provided.

The eight principles that guide the company's actions are: citizenship, customer satisfaction, diversity, employee involvement, financial strength, innovation, integrity, and teamwork (Tribune Company, 2001). In Table 4.3, revenues and assets listed for print, broadcast, and online reflect growth for the media company. The financial standings for 2001 to 2003 are culled from Tribune corporate Web site electronic annual reports and the 10-K reports filed with the Securities and Exchange Commission (SEC, 2001; 2002; 2003).

The 2002 Annual Report: *Leading Markets, Leading Brands* showed 2002 revenues increased to $5.4 billion. By this time, the company owned 26 TV stations, Superstation WGN, WGN radio, and Tribune Entertainment, and 22% ownership in the WB Network, 31% ownership in TV Food Network, and 9% ownership in The Golf Channel. There were 11 newspapers, 5 Hispanic publica-

TABLE 4.3
Tribune Company 2001 Financial Highlights (in thousands)

Operating Revenue	2001	2000	Change
Publishing	$ 3,843,949	$ 3,443,495	
Broadcasting and entertainment	1,349,935	1,465,553	
Interactive	59,482	41,782	
Total revenue	$ 5,253,366	$ 4,950,830	6%

tions, Tribune Media Services, CLTV cable, and 50 Web sites reaching 9 million unique visitors per month.

> The theme of this report—leading marketing, leading brands—defines our strategy and speaks to the unique growth opportunities we're pursuing in the places that matter most to advertisers. These include the top three U.S. markets, New York, Los Angeles and Chicago, where Tribune is the only media company operating newspaper, television stations and websites. (Tribune Company, 2002, p. 1)

The company had a notable year on many fronts, winning three Pulitzer Prizes at the *Los Angles Times* and *Newsday*. The operating cash flow for the year increased 20% to $1.5 billion, and $60 million in incremental revenue was derived from newspaper and cross-media advertising programs. The CareerBuilder.com brand grew as part of online classified advertising appearing in 130 newspapers, insert advertising revenue reached $500 million, and TV news hours were up 41% from 3 years before. Table 4.4 shows a 2% increase in revenues for 2002 from the previous year.

The 2003 Annual Report: *Creating Value: 20 Years as a Public Company* showed 2003 revenues increased again to $5.6 billion. For a 20-year investor, a $100 investment in 1983 with dividends reinvested would translate into $2,151 in 2003 (Tribune Company, 2003). "Tribune's history dates back to 1847, but it was just 20

TABLE 4.4
Tribune Company 2002 Financial Highlights (in thousands)

Operating Revenue	2002	2001	Change
Publishing	$ 3,863,779	$ 3,843,949	
Broadcasting and entertainment	1,443,950	1,349,935	
Interactive	76,699	59,482	
Total revenue	$ 5,384,428	$ 5,253,366	2%

years ago that we became a public company. And as long-term shareholders know, our stock has been a solid investment," according to the introduction of the report (Tribune Company, 2003, p. 1). Creating shareholder value was a top priority for the year and initiatives included:

- Purchased TV stations in St. Louis and Portland.
- Launched *Hoy* in Chicago, an extension of the Spanish-language paper in New York.
- Increased CareerBuilder online revenue share and passed Monster.com as the leader in job postings.
- Accelerated growth of Superstation WGN with new cable and direct broadcast satellite agreements.
- Invested in *amNewYork*, a free newspaper for young Manhattan commuters.
- Achieved a labor agreement at the *Baltimore Sun* that aligns pay with performance. (Tribune Company, 2003, pp. 2–3)

In Table 4.5, a brief look at key economic standing for 2003 reveals continued growth of about 4% for the company. Tribune's Interactive and Publishing businesses were reported separately until the first quarter of 2003. Due to various management and organizational changes, Publishing and Interactive were integrated so that operating results for Interactive business are reported as a

TABLE 4.5
Tribune Company 2003 Financial Highlights (in thousands)

Operating Revenue	2003	2002	Change
Publishing	$ 4,036,920*	$ 3,863,779	
Broadcasting and entertainment	1,557,909	1,443,950	
Interactive	N/A	76,699	
Total revenue	$ 5,594,829	$ 5,384,428	4%

*Interactive revenues included

part of the Publishing business segment (Securities and Exchange Commission, 2003, p. 1).

This review of Tribune's annual reports over the 3 years highlights its economic growth and internal initiatives to expand value. Of interest is that, of the three business segments, publishing has generated more than 70% of revenues. As with any organization, the company has worked to create shareholder growth and economic success. It is apparent, however, in the narrative of the annual reports, that a company goal is converged presentations of content across print, broadcast, and online units. Whether it is the three Pulitzer Prizes won in 2002, the launching of Spanish-language *Hoy* in Chicago, or CareerBuilders.com as a national classified initiative, the company pushes its integrated efforts forward. Converged operations are incorporated in these changes, and the annual reports identify why incremental advertising has occurred through cross-promotions.

Some of the concepts, themes, and trends from the in-depth interviews at the Tribune reflect issues that are on the forefront of convergence. Whether from an organizational or individual perspective, several issues appear to reflect aspects of convergence key to operations in Chicago. Table 4.6 illustrates some of the recurring issues for the convergence process in Chicago.

The Tribune Company case study provides a snapshot of the company and its Chicago operations as it moves forward in the

TABLE 4.6
Chicago Convergence Themes and Trends

Creative	Economic	Individual Perspective	Organizational Perspective
Promotion	Incremental	Professional	Good journalism
Branding	ad revenues	exposure	Conference calls
Special	Advertising	New skills	Joint meetings
projects	New products	Marketability	Utility of content
Newsletters	Business	Cultural change	Profile server
	development	Training	Tribnet
			Sharing content
			Cross-promotion

21st century. The narrative from the in-depth interviews is used to illustrate how the concept and process of convergence are evolving. Numerous changes have occurred over the past 3 years and will continue to do so in years to come. Tribune serves as a traditional convergence pioneer because its performance, operations, and mission reflect a continued surge forward into a world that seeks to integrate technology with mediated messages on air, in print, and online.

REFERENCES

Columbia Journalism Review. (2004). Who owns what. Retrieved June 14, 2004, from http://www.cjr.org/tools/owners/tribune.asp

Haas, T. (2000). Qualitative case study methods in newsroom research and reporting. In S. H. Iorio (Ed.), *Qualitative research in journalism: Taking it to the streets* (pp. 59–73). Mahwah, NJ: Lawrence Erlbaum Associates.

Lindemann, C. (2001, March 19). No payoff yet. After missing a quick payoff, old-media companies look for a winning new-media play. *Broadcasting & Cable, 131*(12), 44–52.

Lipinski, A. M. (2000, October 26). *Roadmap 2005: National vs. regional journalism strategies for a successful future.* Washington, DC: Pew Center for Civic Journalism.

Moses, L. (2001, January 15). Finis for fun and games as online layoffs mount. *Editor & Publisher, 134*(3), 5–6.

Securities and Exchange Commission. (2001). Form 10-K tribune company. Retrieved May 2, 2004, from www.sec.gov

Securities and Exchange Commission. (2002). Form 10-K tribune company. Retrieved May 2, 2004, from www.sec.gov

Securities and Exchange Commission. (2003). Form 10-K tribune company. Retrieved May 2, 2004, from www.sec.gov

Superstation WGN 25th anniversary. (2004, April 5). *Broadcasting & Cable, 134*(14), A2–A14.

Swinging for the fences. (2004, April 5). *Broadcasting & Cable, 134*(14), A4, A6.

Tribune.com (2004). About Tribune: History. Retrieved May 12, 2004, from http://www.tribune.com/about/history/html

Tribune Company. (2001). 2001 Annual Report. Retrieved April 16, 2004, from www.tribune.com

Tribune Company. (2002). 2002 Annual Report. Retrieved April 16, 2004, from www.tribune.com

Tribune Company. (2003).2003 Annual Report. Retrieved April 16, 2004, from www.tribune.com

Tribune Content Sharing. (n.d.) Internal document. Chicago, IL: Tribune Company.

5

Media General: A Temple to Convergence—The News Center in Tampa, Florida

The News Center campus in Tampa, Florida, appears quite ordinary when a visitor approaches the center steps that separate 200 and 202 South Parker Street. However, what has occurred inside the building on the left is far from ordinary—The Tampa Tribune, WFLA-TV, and TBO.com are housed under one roof. The buildings sit on the banks of the Hillsborough River in downtown Tampa and a photographer's bird's eye view from the University of Tampa. In what has been tagged "a temple to convergence," the building houses the parties from a wedding of sorts in 2000 when the separate media entities entered the new building. Since that time, as with any marital arrangement, there have been some relational issues to negotiate, but thus far the marriage of the three business units has found success.

Metaphors aside, The News Center is a laboratory for convergence that is watched by media insiders and outsiders around the country and the world. It is quite ordinary on any given day to see tours of the newsrooms being conducted during the busy production cycles for all three entities. Visitors including academics, professionals, and students, as well as groups from the Poynter Institute, the American Press Institute, and other national and global organizations have traversed through the hallways. Visitors peer over the celebrated three-story atrium with its focal point the multimedia desk on the bottom level in the TV newsroom. The desk is a central location at which members of the various business units can gather to collect or exchange information.

TEMPLE TO CONVERGENCE

The News Center in Tampa is part of parent company Media General's strategy to incorporate converged operations of its disparate business units. The News Center epitomizes this strategy by bringing the print, broadcast, and online units under one roof. Numerous articles have been written and studies conducted on the use of multimedia and the convergence operations in Tampa. It continues to be a laboratory of convergence, demonstrating what will evolve from this multimillion dollar initiative to take the media industry into the 21st century. The approach to analyzing the three case studies in this book is explanation building—an inductive approach that uses the collected data to build an explanation about the case (Haas, 2000). The Tampa operations were chosen for this case study to take a closer look at convergence as both a concept and process at The News Center. The goal is to analyze what has occurred in the past, what strategies are currently in use, and projections for the future. Through participant observation and a series of interviews in 2002 and 2004, the Tampa operation was examined for its use of convergence as a process. The converged operations are a business change, philosophical change, and a change for journalists in the daily practice of their duties.

The holdings of the Richmond, Virginia-based Media General are inclusive of newspapers and TV stations across the southern, southeastern, and western portions of the country. Table 5.1 lists the current holdings using corporate Web sites, *Columbia Journalism Review's* Who Owns What, and other sources.

INNOVATION CHAMPION

In Rogers' (1995) diffusion research within organizations, Gil Thelen, publisher and president of *The Tampa Tribune*, would be labeled an "innovation champion." Rogers' Generalization 10-4 states, "The involvement of an innovation champion contributes to the success of an innovation in an organization" (p. 398). Thelen is

TABLE 5.1
Media General

Newspapers

Florida: The Tampa Tribune, (Sebring) Highlands Today, (Brooksville) Hernando Today, Jackson County Floridan; Virginia: Richmond Times-Dispatch, Bristol Herald Courier, The (Lynchburg) News & Advance, The (Charlottesville) Daily Progress, Potomac (Woodbridge) News, Danville Register & Bee, The (Waynesboro) News Virginian, Manassas Journal Messenger, Culpeper Star-Exponent, Virginia Business; North Carolina: Winston-Salem Journal, (Concord & Kannapolis) Independent Tribune, Hickory Daily Record, Statesville Record & Landmark, The (Morganton) News Herald, The Reidsville Review, The (Eden) Daily News, The (Marion) McDowell News; Alabama: The Dothan Eagle, Opelika-Auburn News, The Enterprise Ledger; South Carolina: The (Florence) Morning News; Colorado: The Denver Post (20%); Washington, D.C.: Media General News Services; and more than 100 weeklies and periodicals

Television

Florida: WFLA-TV- Tampa, WKRG-TV - Mobile, WJWB-TV - Jacksonville, WMBB-TV - Panama City; Alabama: WIAT-TV - Birmingham; Georgia: WJBF-TV - Augusta, WRBL-TV - Columbus, WSAV-TV - Savannah, WNEG-TV - Toccoa; Iowa: KIMT-TV - Mason City; Kansas: KBSD-TV - Dodge City, KBSL-TV - Goodland, KBSH-TV - Hays, KWCH-TV - Wichita; Kentucky: WTVQ-TV - Lexington; Louisiana: KALB-TV - Alexandria; Mississippi: WHLT-TV - Hattiesburg, WJTV-TV - Jackson; North Carolina: WNCT-TV - Greenville; South Carolina: WSPA-TV - Greenville/Spartanburg/Anderson, WASV-TV - Greenville/Spartanburg/Anderson, WCBD-TV - Charleston, WBTW-TV - Florence/Myrtle Beach; Tennessee: WDEF-TV - Chattanooga, WJHL-TV - Johnson City; Virginia: WSLS-TV - Roanoke.

Other

More than 50 online enterprises; Media General Financial Services

an innovation champion because he is a vocal proponent of convergence in Tampa, for Media General, and the industry. He writes and speaks on the topic of convergence or, the term regularly used in Tampa, *multimedia newsroom*. Thelen (2002) once wrote that, for critics, "convergence signifies the corporate homogenization and profit obsession that's gripping publicly held companies," whereas proponents find "convergence is the appropriate business and journalistic response to our customers' increasingly agnostic media usage" (p. 16). Thelen still speaks positively regarding the future of convergence even though he contends that he shies from predicting the future of convergence in the industry.

The News Center has evolved from Thelen's early statements into a convergence operation where multimedia is key to daily operations. The operative word used by Thelen and others is *collaboration*—convergence is about collaboration among the three business units in the Tampa building. First, that collaboration stems from an understanding of the separate and converged purposes of the business units. The pertinent question raised regarding convergence is whether we receive multiple opinions or whether we receive one opinion across three platforms. The mantra in Tampa is that each business unit is guided by independent decisions, but collaboratively working together across the platforms. According to Thelen:

> We have separate decision structures on the three platforms, the news judgments are made independently although the information gathering is done collaboratively. I think the key thing here is how many feet you have on the street. If what had happened here, is that we reduced the number of journalists gathering information, then I think the case can be made that convergence was diminishing voices. But, we have more people on the streets that we did four years ago. (personal communication, April 2, 2004)

Most of the discussion and documentation on the rules of engagement for the practice of convergence suggest that the information must be distributed on a timely basis. In Tampa that entails that "we publish on the first available printing press" (G. Thelen, personal communication, April 2, 2004).

Organizational cultural changes are a challenge for any organization, but in print and broadcast newsrooms it is particularly salient. In a video produced in 2000 on convergence and taped in Tampa by the McNeil Lehrer Hour, correspondent Terrence Smith spoke to WFLA-TV anchor Gayle Sierens. Sierens recalled a story in which she taped an interview with an accused murderer; instead of first airing it on the TV station, she wrote a story for the newspaper. In the video, Sierens talked about scooping herself on the story, stating that it was a cultural change for her as a broadcaster in a converged environment. Thelen expanded on the topic of cultural change when he spoke of the sports department in Tampa:

> We still have huge cultural and organizational challenges to meet. As an example we now have a single sports staff, but face questions such as what is being first now mean in an instant information environment? If a Tribune sports reporter is breaking "his/her" exclusive Tampa Bay Buccaneers story on the 11 o'clock news, what frequently happens is it gives time to hobble together some type of story that they can put into the newspaper. So have we injured ourselves by publishing on one platform that takes away competitive advantage from another platform? We are still working through that question. Because while the ultimate mantra here is that the community owns the story.... We still have an engrained professional, competitive instinct that says my story in my medium and that is what being first means. So we have to deal with the scooping yourself question without stamping out the wonderful competitive desire to beat the competition. (G. Thelen, personal communication, April 2, 2004)

Thus, collaboration translates into telling the story and delivering it on the first "printing" press or platform that is available. This is a challenge for some current staffers and even more so for potential journalists. The issue raised for academics teaching future journalists is how to prepare them for work in a converged environment. There are basics such as knowing how to write, knowing news values, possessing ethics, and having a specialty, but equally important is an understanding of a multimedia environment. Thelen took this one step further, adding what he considers four important steps for future journalists:

> Number one: The number one thing they need to come out of j-school (journalism) with is craft competence. Craft competence as a reporter. Craft competence as a copy editor. Craft competence in (any area).

> Number two: They have to have an understanding of this multimedia world. A real appreciation for the rapidly changing world that we are in.

Number three: They have to have the willingness and capacity to acquire new skills along the way. And just know that this is going to be
an adventure in lifelong learning.

Number four: Increasingly, this work is about groups of people getting things done. Rather than have the individual practitioner going
off in a corner and doing it themselves. (G. Thelen, personal communication, April 2, 2004)

Convergence does not operate in a vacuum and, as discussed in
chapter 1, the term dated from the 17th and 18th centuries and derived from many disciplines before becoming a part of the vernacular in the popular press by the 1990s (Gordon, 2003). During a
2004 interview, Thelen noted that his preliminary experience with
convergence and collaboration occurred in 1990 in North
Carolina. At that time, he brought together a consortium of universities, TV stations, and newspapers for a town hall meeting to discuss reforming state government. Thelen recalls that event as one
in which an understanding was created that the separate entities
would be stronger if they worked together. "I think that what kept
us apart was regulatory. What kept us apart was ownership. What
kept us apart were some outdated notions about competition.
What kept us apart was our fundamental blind spot about collaboration" (personal communication, April 2, 2004).

In Tampa, the business units have worked to clear up this blind
spot. Collaboration occurs daily across units despite wrinkles
and bumps that need smoothing from corporate culture to delivery platform. A marketing campaign launched in 2003 at *The
Tampa Tribune* illustrates the expanding approach to the converged environment.

LIFE. PRINTED DAILY.

Amy Chown, marketing director for *The Tampa Tribune*, during a
2004 interview explained the new campaign, *Life. Printed Daily.*
as a foray into connecting more with the audience. The campaign

has brought newsroom journalists and the business side staff together in promoting the work they do every day. In a page one letter to readers in *The Tampa Tribune* in 2003, Thelen wrote:

> Life. Printed Daily.
>
> The Tampa Tribune is unveiling a branding campaign this week highlighted by those three words. Let me explain how they relate the Tribune's work to you. A newspaper represents a daily account of events, trends and issues that touch people's lives. Not every story relates to every reader, but pictures, words or graphics can connect residents with the larger world and give them tools for understanding and action.... No other medium provides this information like a quality local newspaper. It's easy to get, carry around and use. It's where you weigh what's happening around you and discover how it intersects with your life. And it's served up every day. So somehow, in some way, for Tribune readers, it's their life. Printed daily. So it's not just a slogan. It's our commitment to you every day that we deliver relevant, meaningful and useful content. Our aim is for you to find your life reflected in our pages and in our new marketing campaign. (Thelen, 2003, p. A1)

From business cards, stationery, and reporters' notebooks (see Figs. 5.1 and 5.2), to graphics on delivery trucks, newspapers, and billboards, the new slogan taps into the direction in which the company is pointing. Chown contended that branding is often misunderstood, especially if a company jumps to slogans without understanding exactly what the company means to its

Todd L. Chappel Senior Editor/Photography
phone: 813-259-7873   fax: 813-259-7676
e-mail: tchappel@tampatrib.com
photo: 813-259-7685

THE TAMPA TRIBUNE
LIFE. PRINTED DAILY.
TBO.com
200-202 S. Parker Street, Tampa, FL 33606-2395

Fig. 5.1. Printed with permission by The Tampa Tribune.

Fig. 5.2. Printed with permission by The Tampa Tribune.

customers. Chown and others at the Tribune spent 2 years on research and development before arriving at the new slogan. Also a communication audit was conducted with the paper's external audience through every form of communication (e.g., news articles, photographs, inhouse ads, correspondence, billboards) that might be received from the company to ascertain how the organization was viewed. Chown wanted to learn what made people tick in the community, what issues they identified with, and how they viewed the organization. "It is all about the content and connectivity to the community" (A. Chown, personal communication, April 2, 2004). She contended that for convergence to work an organization must have good journalism, must be relevant to the consumer in a meaningful way, and must have a collaborative effort. According to Chown, the acceptance of the branding campaign by journalists in the newsroom signified the ultimate acceptance that it was not just a slogan, but a part of the company's mission—a mission that includes daily practices that lead to working together on all three platforms, from presentation of content of the Tampa Bay Buccaneers to overcoming challenges to successfully integrate daily operations.

TECHNOLOGY CHALLENGES AND BUDGETBANK

An early organizational cultural challenge was the use of terminology from broadcast to print. In print, the word *budget* means the content to be produced by the newspaper for the day, rather than economic issues that might creep into the minds of broadcasters. That was an early semantic challenge and one that Tampa has easily surpassed. The separate business units kept their own budgets or lists of content to be used daily. This was a challenge because even inside the newspaper separate text files and memos contained pieces of information on what was available for content. Tampa needed a content management system that would allow the business units to share the same information. BudgetBank is a database software that allows the staff at the print, broadcast, and online units to speak the same language.

Allyn DiVito is a senior editor at *The Tampa Tribune*. DiVito and a computer programmer at Media General's headquarters developed BudgetBank. The database is housed on servers outside of the Richmond, Virginia, headquarters of the company. DiVito shares an interesting story about the development and use of BudgetBank at The News Center in Tampa (personal communication, July 16, 2002).

BudgetBank is a Web-based software system first developed for use in Tampa and expanded to include the Florida publishing group and, eventually, all Media General publishing units. BudgetBank (see Fig. 5.3) allows users to fill out a template to place proposed content on a system that everyone at the organization can access. The site is restricted with a firewall to employees who are provided a user log-in. Once logged in, a profile takes the user to the place in the software system where he or she needs to go. A print or broadcast reporter would be taken to their vari-

WFLA
BUDGET SCHEDULE

News Channel 8
on your side

Shoot Date	Air Date	Arrival Time	Slug	Reporter / Producer / Photog
7/15/2002	7/19/2002	12:15 p.m., Superdesk	VOICE	Bearden, Michelle _Same as, reporter Unassigned, TV Photog

Newscast: 5:30 PM

We go to the home of Hugh Burns...who is starting the tampa bay area's first chapter of Voice of the Faith..the national movement bringing Catholic lay people together who are sick of church hierarchy and the current sex scandal. This group is picking up steam all over the country..we find out why these Catholics would rather work from within than leave.
Location: Sun City Center
Directions: I've got them...I'll meet photog at Superdesk at 12:15 p.m. Monday
Contacts: hugh burns
Breakout: n
Internet: n
Added--: Bearden, Michelle 7/12/2002 1:42:00 PM

Enterprise

7/19/2002	7/16/2002	ALL DAY	ASTHMA-EDIT	Maher, Irene Unassigned, producer Webb, Jim

Newscast: , Unassigned

JIM EDITS ASTHMA TARGET STORY FOR MONDAY'S PHONE BANK.
Location: STATION
Directions: N/A
Contacts: IRENE
Added--: Maher, Irene 7/16/2002 4:27:00 PM

Enterprise

7/19/2002	7/16/2002	9 AM	HEART-SCREENING	Maher, Irene Unassigned, producer Webb, Jim

Newscast: , Unassigned

LOCAL DOCTOR REACTS TO NEW AHA STUDY WHICH SAYS SCREENING FOR HEART DISEASE SHOULD BEGIN IN THE 20'S.
Location: HYDE PARK
Directions: N/A
Contacts: Sara,
Added--: Maher, Irene 7/16/2002 4:21:00 PM

7/19/2002	7/19/2002		8OYS-VICKI719	Lim, Victoria Unassigned, producer Unassigned, TV Photog

Newscast: , Unassigned

i need a photog to shoot a standup with me at the airport (kate is with stacie and has a busted ankle)

need to write murillo - couldn't do it yesterday because of day of story
Added--: Lim, Victoria 7/18/2002 4:55:00 PM

7/19/2002	7/19/2002		AD WATCH	UnAssigned, Reporter Famiano, Maureen UnAssigned, Photog

Newscast: , Unassigned

We could do another 8 on your side voice of the voter Ad Watch. There are 2 new ones paid for by the GOP for Jeb now running. Interesting to note, one features our buddy, our pal- Manatee County sheriff Charlie Wells.
I have the text of both and have gotten permission to run them from the GOP. There are more claims in these, it may take some time to verify the facts.
Added--: Famiano, Maureen 7/18/2002 3:58:00 PM

7/19/2002	7/19/2002	9:45 a.m.	CLEARWATER MARINE AQUARIUM	Guyardo, Gayle _Same as, reporter _Same as, reporter

Newscast: Morning

Fig. 5.3. Budget schedule. Printed with permission by WFLA-TV News Channel 8.

ous areas. An editor, photographer, or producer's user profile would follow the same process.

"This page looks a little bit complicated, really all it's asking you is what you want to display.... Think about all those budgets that were fragmented and all these different drawers and file cabinets and electronic places that you had to look in, and you had to know where something was to find it. So there were no search capabilities on those files" (A. DiVito, personal communication, July 16, 2002). The new software changes that process.

BudgetBank is a structured query language (SQL) database in which any field is searchable. SQL is a standard language for using a database in a network environment. What is available with BudgetBank is content information from TV, the Web, newspaper, or photo, whatever is needed from all of the divisions in one location. For example, a newspaper page designer laying out a Feature section knows what is available, the length, and any accompanying photos or graphics. Meanwhile, an employee of the TV station can ascertain whether the content proposed for the newspaper Feature section has a possibility for collaboration with broadcast. According to DiVito, BudgetBank was built from the inside out by talking to people who would use it and determining what they would need in identifying content. There are mandatory areas of the template that require completion so that everyone views key components of the content. The date and run date are listed, as well as the length for broadcast or print stories and ranking of stories. An icon of a camera or artist table is automatically generated if photos or graphics are available. Also the reporter's name and number and the editor or producer's contact information are documented for ease of use. DiVito's background as a photographer contributed to his thinking in framed sections, so a user can print out a text of a budget item with all the pertinent information. Tampa's photographers are mobile, with digital cell phones and laptops in their cars. They can access the information they need on the run and get to assignments knowing more of what to expect. This provides immediate connectivity to people in the office to transmit the photographers' work.

DAILY COLLABORATION

TBO.com or Tampa Bay Online is an example of Media General's commitment to convergence. Peter Howard, Team Leader, News & Special Projects, said TBO.com became its own company in January 2000, which created a third division at the Tampa facility (personal communication, July 16, 2002). Parent company Media General now supports a publishing division, broadcast division, and interactive division. In 2002, there were approximately 25 employees at TBO.com, distributed evenly between content and marketing. Howard joined the company in 2000 after a redesign and has been instrumental in efforts to integrate content across the units. Howard identified four tools that the online unit specifically addresses: news, sports, weather, and entertainment. In Florida, weather is an important issue, and content from the other three units is often collaborative on issues of weather. For example, a special section on the 2002 hurricane season produced by *The Tampa Tribune* was linked to content with TBO.com and WFLA-TV. The audience was provided with multiple avenues to access pertinent information on weather concerns in the area. The 12-page broadsheet was filled with news coverage, evacuation information, shelters, and other resources. All of this information was cross-promoted with WFLA-TV and TBO.com for continuous coverage and live updates.

Howard points to the year 2000 as pivotal in many ways for the convergence operation, from weather coverage to the controversy over presidential election ballots in Florida.

> We had a couple of events in 2000 that really defined what we were all about. There was a big fire in the entertainment district in Tampa that burned an apartment complex that took up a couple of blocks. But the one event that really helped define what we were doing, I think, was the presidential elections. It was 36 days of hell. We recorded, at the time, what was our highest traffic numbers for a day during that time. (P. Howard, personal communication, July 16, 2002)

The pace continues to quicken as the TBO.com staff continuously works to update content and connect audiences on all platforms.

When the *Tribune* went through a redesign in 2001, an internal document entitled *Tampa Tribune Redesign: Collaborative Story Planning, Readers and You* stated that three requirements of staff were key to the success of the planning: that they consistently put readers' convenience and gratification above their own; that they take initiative to produce a better paper for readers, not relying on others to do so; and that they work in a collaborative fashion on the 10 or 12 most promising stories of the day (Tampa Tribune Redesign, n.d.). The collaboration push is based on growth in the Tampa Bay area and the newspaper's efforts to be relevant and reach the reader. Collaboration entails constant communication across units regarding the daily content, what is being used, when it will be used, how, and for what reason. The ongoing question is where convergence can play an effective role in the presentation of content.

Representatives from the three business units conduct a daily pulse check on collaborative opportunities in Tampa. During *The Tampa Tribune's* morning budget meeting, representatives from different areas of the newspaper, TBO.com, and WFLA-TV review the BudgetBank listings for the day and discuss the possibilities that exist for collaboration. They then use a scorecard of the various sections of the newspaper, which are graded to ascertain where integration of content successfully occurred. The card is really a series of pieces of paper that are used to address specific concerns about the content that was used the previous day. A scorecard is placed on the conference room bulletin board for Page 1A, Metro, BayLife/Flavor, Friday Extra, Sunday Moneysense, Monday Moneysense, Daily Moneysense, and Sports. How does this work? Someone goes to the board and fills out each applicable card with input from those present at the meeting. It is a conscious effort on the part of editors, managers, and team leaders. The scoring process is a specific action that can be attributed to an observation of commitment to convergence. The cards include questions that have a place to circle "yes" or "no" to identify the action (see Table 5.2).

This scoring exercise creates daily conversations about convergence within and among the three business units. In chapter 1, we

TABLE 5.2
Page 1A Scorecard

DATE_____   PAGE 1A SCORECARD

(Circle One)

YES   NO   Do we have local stories and photographs on the front? How
           many _____?

YES   NO   Does the front page include coverage of our top 10 community
           issues? How many _____?

YES   NO   Is our writing lively, engaging, active?

YES   NO   Was the centerpiece a successful product of collaboration?
           ✓ for yes, X for no _____story _____headline _____design
           _____photography _____graphics

YES   NO   Did we collaborate two stories?

YES   NO   Did we break news?

YES   NO   Did we hold a story (stories) to the front? How many _____?

YES   NO   Did we maximize our multimedia opportunities? If not, what did we
           miss _____?

YES   NO   Did we have an accurate and fair report, free of errors?

YES   NO   Did the section reflect the diversity of our community in terms of
           sources, issues, photographs and events?

YES   NO   Did the writer and photographer work together?

YES   NO   Did we use accurate, easy-to-read graphics?

Printed with permission by The Tampa Tribune.

discussed the Seven Observations of Convergence, which included communication, cooperation, commitment, and the customer. The constant communication allows all parties to keep the dialogue going on what integrated content means for the organization. In Tampa, the cooperation is necessary daily for the separate business units to understand what each is doing and where the efforts on integrating content should focus. The exercise with the scorecard at each daily meeting illustrates the organization's commitment to convergence. These efforts are being conducted to ensure that the customer is receiving the message and types of content identified as applicable for their use. Such internal processes support efforts that keep convergence on the front burner in the organization. They all illustrate a top—down imperative that convergence as a concept and process is how the company does business.

The Tampa convergence laboratory serves as an example of daily commitment to integrate content from business units and maintain the distinctions of each platform. The TV station has components that are unique to a broadcaster and collaborates in areas that should enhance the opportunities for all parties.

WFLA-TV, NEWS CHANNEL 8

Forrest Carr is the News Director at WFLA-TV News Channel 8 and an active participant in the convergence process in Florida. Carr is no stranger to a changing culture in broadcast newsrooms as well as the process of generating and distributing content through the process of convergence. Carr (2002a) wrote about convergence from his perspective and the issues he deems important to making the process work or not work. He noted that, at The News Center, it is an evolving process that continues to shape and reshape itself. "The Tampa model of convergence, a cooperative arrangement between three co-owned media partners, is voluntary and is carried out in such a way as to preserve editorial independence for all three partners" (Carr, 2002a, par. 6). Carr identified seven basic levels of convergence he feels are critical to making the process work in Tampa: daily tips and information, spot news, photography, enterprise reporting, franchises, events, and public service (Carr,

2002b). He views these areas as important to the ongoing conversation on what will work in the converged environment. In Carr's view, all content on the broadcast platform or the other two does not necessitate integration. Instead, he pursues convergence where those efforts make the most sense.

For example, with enterprise reporting, a WFLA reporter could develop a story for broadcast that has multimedia implications. Integrating the content with the newspaper could mean additional content or how-to or tips that could be cut out of the paper. TBO.com could be used for video and further aspects of a story that the audience could view at any time after the initial broadcast for further information.

The News Center Pledge in Tampa (see Fig. 5.4) is an internal document that provides a guideline for handling the convergence process across units. Tampa considers convergence a voluntary component for all parties. The News Center Pledge begins with a commitment to "the highest standards of quality and ethics" and identifies the fact that all three units are jointly owned but make "independent news decisions" (The News Center Pledge, n.d.). The Pledge identifies six issues that *The Tampa Tribune*, WFLA-TV News Channel 8, and TBO.com are committed to accomplishing for the community in presentation of its content. This document provides a tool to help understand what the three units work to make happen at The News Center.

The News Channel 8 Statement of Philosophy (see Fig. 5.5) identifies five key issues to which the broadcaster is committed for its viewers: viewer advocacy; solutions; relevance, fairness, and accuracy; accountability; and self-accountability. The philosophy statement creates an open dialogue with the public to create a scorecard for WFLA. In this era of convergence, it is apparent that media entities need to communicate with their external constituency. The emerging technologies have increased the channels of accessibility to information. That a broadcast or print outlet is the primary source cannot be assumed. Any effort by a media entity to communicate with the audience creates an opportunity for dialogue and understanding of the process.

The News Center Pledge

We, at The News Center, hold ourselves to the highest standards of quality and ethics. While *The Tampa Tribune*, News Channel 8, and TBO.com are owned jointly, we make independent news decisions. Together, we make this commitment to the citizens of our community:

*   We will provide timely and relevant news and information. We will present the news accurately, fairly and in context.

*   When we make a mistake, we will correct it promptly.

*   We will give voice to the voiceless and reflect the full diversity of life in the Tampa Bay area.

*   We will serve as watchdogs for our community, exposing problems and exploring solutions. We will hold the powerful accountable.

*   We will conduct ourselves with compassion and sensitivity to privacy.

*   We expect you to hold us accountable.

If you have questions or concerns about our news coverage, call 1-800-527-2758, e-mail us at voice@TBO.com or write to Citizens' Voice, The News Center, 200 S. Parker St., Tampa FL 33606-2395.

FIG. 5.4.   Printed with permission by WFLA-TV News Channel 8.

Carr (2002b) stated that, in addition to the TV station's daily meetings to discuss content, a broadcast representative attends the newspaper's meeting to collaborate on convergence opportunities. A multimedia liaison who attends all these meetings serves as a connector to maximize moments where integration of content can occur. Ken Knight is the Multimedia Editor who serves as this liaison. Knight is busy moving from the multimedia desk on the first floor of the atrium in the TV newsroom to the newspaper and TBO.com. Knight described his role across the business units:

Statement of Philosophy

Final Draft

Viewer Advocacy
We at News Channel 8 will be advocates for our viewers. This means we will help empower them to improve their lives and community, to hold the powerful accountable and to ensure the voice of the public is heard in the process of setting public policy. News Channel 8 will ask the tough questions, dig hard for facts and push hard for answers. Enterprise reporting lies at the heart of this commitment.

Solutions
The desire to spotlight solutions, not simply to find problems, will inspire our journalism. We will help people directly when possible and appropriate. We will give voice to a wide range of viewpoints and ideas. We will seek opportunities to provide forums for community conversation, discussion and deliberation.

Relevance, Fairness and Accuracy
We will seek stories that are relevant to our viewers, provide viewer benefit and add value to their lives. We will tell the stories necessary to show t..e full fabric of life in our communities, and to portray those communities and the people who live there in a fair and accurate light.

Accountability
We will hold those with power, responsibility and influence accountable. This includes elected public officials; non-elected civil servants, educators and law enforcement officials; businesses; public figures; and any that hold or seek power and influence.

Self-Accountability
News Channel 8 subscribes to the RTNDA and SPJ codes of ethics, which require journalists to seek the truth and report it, to minimize harm, to act independently and to be accountable. We will hold ourselves accountable to the public by stating publicly what we stand for and by providing a mechanism for the public to hold us to it. We will continually evaluate our performance in light of our stated principles and will invite the public to participate in this process. We will admit mistakes and promptly take the appropriate steps to correct them.

Summary
The desire to serve our viewers will drive us. We will dedicate ourselves to this goal with passion, vigor and a sense of urgency. We will reach out to and join with our viewers when appropriate to fulfill these goals. We will open a dialogue with them to ensure our accountability. We will meet, in the fullest manner possible, the promise contained in our slogan, "On Your Side."

FIG. 5.5. Printed with permission by WFLA-TV News Channel 8.

I bring them together so they can compare notes, they can hold conversations.... When I was growing up in college this (would be) completely against everything we know as journalists to share information. What I was told in the street, I came back and reported on the print side ... there was no way I was going to share. So that's one of the cultural changes that I think has come over the years, that initially I'm sure many journalists on the broadcast and the print side were uncomfortable with. We had been competitive though we were owned by the same company. And I think convergence had occurred years prior to coming into this building, but on a managerial level. It was managers calling each other and saying, "Hey, we have the story, what do you guys have?"... It had never really impacted the majority of reporters. (K. Knight, personal communication, July 17, 2002)

That connection has expanded since the early days. Knight said for the majority of reporters, the convergence operations are not so much a shock, but a new cultural regime. For some that was a great challenge, and for others an organizational cultural change continues to unfold. Knight suggested that some journalists were able to make the change more readily than others. There are numerous print and TBO.com reporters doing stand-alone interviews for the TV stations. Several broadcasters now routinely convert their work to print stories or for online presentation. Knight called the changes in presentation "layering the news." From each platform, the audience can connect with a different aspect of the content.

What you get on WFLA in a minute thirty package is restricted by that minute thirty. If you want to get more depth, of course, you're going to go to the newspaper. To get even greater depth, you're going to go to TBO because it has multimedia elements.... So I consider what we do here a layering of the news. It's not a replication. (K. Knight, personal communication, July 17, 2002)

Knight admitted that reaching this point in the process has included a learning curve. In the early days at The News Center, print reporters were put on air, according to Knight. This was not the best tactic because of time and because some print reporters were not trained in or accustomed to the needs of broadcast. Lessons learned include placing the best person in the best place for presentation of content. Often the better method is to share content, wherein a print reporter writes a story and shares components that broadcast and online can use to add another dimension. Knight believes it is important to prepare reporters, especially if a print reporter is asked to go on air. "One of the things that I've discovered in my time in this position is the most critical things for print journalists is to know what they're being asked. Because what happens if they are cold—they stumble and they stammer—and the reporter's ability is at stake" (K. Knight, personal communication, July 17, 2002). Knight does not want to see anyone unprepared and feels that preparation for the three platforms is a key to success for convergence practices.

In Knight's view, his role is that of a facilitator to help make things work in the converged environment. The information he gleans from all parties can be shared to help with the presentation of content. Knight contended that no one is forced to go on air if they are from print, but managers and editors have started to identify people comfortable with multimedia work. With preparation and training, multimedia will become more a part of the process for journalists. "So one of the new deals is when you come into the paper you're going to have to—or even on the broadcast side, you have to be willing to converge. You must have that part of your job" (K. Knight, personal communication, July 17, 2002).

In one example of the flexibility in understanding the converged aspects of what occurs in Tampa, a photographer covered a bank robbery in which a police officer was shot. The photographer had a video camera on hand and was able to shoot video footage for WFLA, and frames were later captured for use in the newspaper. Senior Editors Todd Chappel and Joe Brown stated that the more than 23 full-time photographers are often called videographers because they carry digital cell phones, digital cameras, and digital video cameras on assignment. These mobile photographers are equipped with digital technology that makes gathering and disseminating content more efficient.

Chappel and Brown have the opportunity to watch life unfold daily through the lenses of photographers at *The Tampa Tribune*. They work to ensure that visuals are available for content to help tell a story. For Chappel, the impact of convergence has been to move beyond photographers shooting a still for the newspaper, to identifying what is visual enough for moving pictures and video. Brown made it clear that consideration must not only be given to getting stills back to the paper, but the most economic way to deliver the tape if video is shot. Through use of the bureau system tapes can be dropped off for feed to the main office. Priorities must be set with regard to video or stills and which is important to get processed first and ready for presentation. This will change due to the subject mater and conditions. A couple of years ago, a third of the photographers carried video cameras along with still cameras; by 2004, the process accelerated to include all photographers. Convergence is a cultural change for photographers. Brown stated:

> Almost like any change, you have those who embrace it wholeheartedly and you have those who it takes a little while to get them to focus on it, and I think we've done a pretty good job here. A lot of people have embraced it and more jump on board as we go along, but this is a continual learning process for you, for WFLA, who are shooting stills for us sometimes. We have to consider our skill level on both sides. I mean, they have to consider our skill levels when we're being asked to shoot video. They're not typically asking us to shoot a whole package of something. Now we have some photographers that could do that, but across the board not every photographer has the ability to shoot and package a video. (personal communication, July 15, 2002)

Chappell added that he does not look to WFLA to send anyone to shoot stills for a newspaper centerpiece. There may be opportunities where broadcast has something that might be useful for both platforms. The process has to be worked through collaboration and communication on what is applicable. There are no assumptions. *The Tribune* has a photo assignment editor on the multimedia desk who communicates regularly with the TV station.

Chappell said this allows for regular contact if the broadcaster is going to use his helicopter and what work can be shared, or if a photographer can shoot video at an event for the TV stations.

MARKETING AND BUSINESS

Convergence does not operate in a vacuum of the print, broadcast, and online newsrooms in Tampa. Marketing and promoting convergence to the audience and advertisers is essential. Clifford Fewel, Integrated Marketing Solutions Manager at The News Center, is aware of the imperative for understanding the needs of the three platforms. Fewel discussed components of the convergence process in a telephone interview on July 22, 2002. Fewel's business card includes the logo of all three entities, and he considers the card a marketing tool as he seeks to educate customers of the potential opportunities with convergence. He focuses on reaching advertisers by highlighting the importance of integrating the three units. For example, Fewel could provide an automobile dealer with a converged advertising package that includes a spot on WFLA-TV, inclusion in *The Tribune* classifieds, and placement on TBO.com. Fewel's goal is to look for nontraditional avenues to bring to the multimedia platforms. In 2002, Fewel added new sales staff to move convergence forward for reaching advertisers for the three units. Numerous internal challenges existed, according to Fewel, such as setting up one billing system for multimedia clients, but he does not view them as insurmountable.

Ted Stasney of Market Development identified some of the marketing research in the area that specifically addresses integrated operations (personal communication, July 18, 2002). Stasney's data reveal that measurements in the designated market area (DMA) of Tampa Bay in 2000 showed a 17% convergence awareness, which has steadily increased. The special hurricane guide in 2002 is an example of a successful convergence project. The guide was printed in *The Tampa Tribune*, WFLA-TV contributed and promoted with the weather center, and the publication was accessible on TBO.com. Advertisers and the audience were reached across the platforms, with content pivotal to the coastal area of Florida.

"The brands are so strong here, we do not want to dilute with the umbrella of The News Center and cut down that brand equity that exists" (T. Stasney, personal communication, July 18, 2002). Stasney considers the challenge for converged operations to be finding the best use of resources that benefit the user, audience, or reader in Tampa. The potential for cross-promotion is unlimited, Stasney contends, but efforts must be made for the best fit.

At WFLA-TV, Bradley Moses, director of marketing, echoes similar cautions in moving forward with convergence (personal communication, July 18, 2002). Moses' push has been to slowly integrate the powers of partnerships. In 2002, for example, image spots planned to promote the TV station incorporated aspects of convergence and cross-promotion. Moses contended that branding is about perception and the manner in which the organization is viewed. For Moses, convergence presents an opportunity to provide a different service, but needs to be mutually beneficial to all parties.

From an economic vantage point, Media General is fairing well with convergence. In 2003, Ron Redfern, president of Florida Communication Group, joined the three business units in Tampa as a senior executive focusing on the continued development of the three units. The corporate parent's three divisions—publishing, broadcast, and interactive—have been progressing in various markets, and specifically in Tampa. A summary of 3 years of annual reports—from 2001 to 2003—reveals a steady movement in economic improvement for the company. Although 2001 was a tough year because of the dot.com bust and decreased advertising across the country, the company moved forward. The company attributed cost-control measures to address reduced revenues of $807.2 million in 2001 compared with $830.6 million in 2000. Stewart Bryan, chairman and CEO of Media General, in his letter to shareholders, offset the losses by identifying gains in publishing and broadcasting as well as the launch of the interactive division to focus on product and content development.

The 2001 annual report, *Convergence: The Power of Multimedia*, includes discussion of the 2000 debut of The News Center. The document defines *media convergence* as "a separate strategy that promotes cooperation among newspapers, television stations and online enterprises" (Media General, 2001, p. 6). The convergence strategy started in Tampa at The News Center now incorporates business properties in other markets. The annual report's section on Convergence: The Power of Three stated:

> The opportunity to work together across three media platforms in one building was unprecedented, and journalists from all three newsrooms made the most of it. They quickly demonstrated that they could combine their unique strengths to find better ways to gather and present the news of the Tampa Bay area. TBO.com had the ability to break news on a moment's notice, WFLA could follow up with dramatic coverage on its newscasts, and *The Tampa Tribune* could tell the whole story with greater depth in the morning newspaper. (Media General, 2001, p. 8)

The fruits of such efforts for advertisers included reaching audiences through one or combined mediums. The initial multimedia sales included $6.4 million in incremental revenue, with $3.5 million to be realized in 2001 and the rest over the next 3 years. In 2001, the company boasted 25 newspapers in the Southeast, more than 100 periodicals, and 25% interest in *The Denver Post*. Media General owned 26 network-affiliated TV stations, listing WFLA-TV in Tampa as the No. 1 station in Florida (Media General, 2001). The company also owned more than 50 online enterprises. Table 5.3 highlights 2001 financial revenues for Media General.

The 2002 annual report: *A Growing Multimedia Company—Serving the Southeast With High-Quality News, Information, and Entertainment*, focused on shareholder value and

TABLE 5.3
Media General Financials 2001

Revenue	2001	2000	Change
Publishing	$541.3 million	$559.9 million	
Broadcast	$257.6 million	$262.8 million	
Interactive	$8.3 million	$7.9 million	
Total	$807.2 million	$830.6 million	−2.8%

growth opportunities in the Southeast. By this time the Tampa News Center had been in operation for 2 years. Table 5.4 reflects revenue growth in 2002 of $836.8 million from $807.2 million in 2001. Revenue across the divisions improved, however, Media General and other media companies experience the effects of economic conditions across the country in 2001 post-9/11.

The revenue increase in 2002 varied across divisions. Retail advertising was down and publishing felt that change, but the company contends that its cost-control efforts were used to offset revenue decreases. The Interactive Media Division revenues grew 28% in 2002. J. Stewart Bryan, chairman and CEO, emphasized the commitment to building shareholder value in the Southeast where most of the corporate parent's properties are located (Media General, 2002). However, the power of convergence stays at the forefront in discussion of multimedia arrangements that extend from the Tampa market to five new areas. Bryan stated that practicing good journalism across various platforms is possible as "TV station staffs can access the depth of a newspaper's archives, its research capabilities, and the expertise of beat reporters. Newspapers can benefit from a TV station's capabilities for subjects like weather and consumer advocacy. A web site can draw content from both the newspaper and TV partners while also providing original, real-time information and other interactive services" (cited in Media General, 2002, p. 3).

The 2003 annual report, *Media General Integrity, Quality, Innovation: Our Core Values Drive Value*, continued to identify the company's advances. The 2003 revenues were $837.4 million, an

TABLE 5.4
Media General Financials 2002

Revenue	2002	2001	Change
Publishing	$527 million	$541.3 million	
Broadcast	298 million	257.6 million	
Interactive	11.2 million	8.3 million	
Total	$836.8 million	$807.2 million	3.6%

incremental growth from $836.8 million in 2002, as seen in Table 5.5 (Media General, 2003). The chairman cited revenue and audience growth for 2003 despite the war in Iraq and other economic factors. Although the publishing and broadcasting divisions sought to control growth, no substantial revenue growth occurred. Publishing was second among its peer group in total revenue and circulation growth. Broadcasting sought new advertising growth initiatives because of the 2002 lack of political revenue. The Interactive Media Division was down in actual numbers, although recognized for 60% percent revenue growth. Chairman and CEO Bryan stated that 2004 should be optimistic for the company due to the summer Olympics and advertising from the presidential campaign. Revenues from each division did not make significant changes.

SUMMARY

Corporate parent Media General has not experienced revenue windfalls, but shows some incremental growth as reflected in the 3 years of annual reports. A corporate Web site video of the annual meeting in 2004 suggests that Media General has proved that "convergence makes sense journalistically" by improving the quality of the product. Of the six markets where convergence is operating, Tampa is viewed as the most advanced. Whether it is the daily process of integrating content, journalists sharing information, managers planning projects, or marketing campaigns educating the audience, convergence is at the forefront. Pat Mitchell, presentation senior editor, has watched this change

TABLE 5.5
Media General Financials 2003

Revenue	2003	2002	Change
Publishing	$544 million	$527 million	
Broadcast	286 million	298 million	
Interactive	10 million	11.2 million	
Total	$837.4 million	$836.8 million	0.7%

occur and suggests there are more to come as the organization continues to expand on its commitment to the convergence process (personal communication, July 16, 2002). The organizational cultural change and other internal structures are apparent. The third-floor newspaper newsroom has taken on a different look. Different departments are grouped by copy editors, managers, reporters, graphics, features, and photographers. Another phenomenon is the mobility created with the increased use of laptops instead of PCs at each desk. Since the 1980s, newsrooms have had a different look and sound without the clatter of typewriters as computers and other digital technologies have expanded capabilities for collecting, creating, and disseminating content. With the laptops, the atmosphere has changed to one of increased mobility and operations at whatever point a journalist is located. Here technology plays the role of providing flexibility in working conditions for the staff. For example, because photographers have laptops and cell phones in their cars, the need to scramble for information has been reduced (J. Brown, personal communication, July 15, 2002).

There are common themes, trends, and concepts that can be gleaned from the in-depth interviews, observations, and documents collected over the past 3 years in Tampa as illustrated in Table 5.6. From an individual and organizational perspective, some issues stand out as important in the evolution of convergence in Tampa at The News Center.

A day in the life of convergence at The News Center not only entails multimedia use of content, but is multifaceted in its approach. The day begins when each business unit gathers editors, reporters, and other representatives to discuss the content on hand. The advent of the BudgetBank software is an example of improved communication facilitated by technology on a shared space. The print, broadcast, and online units have an enhanced awareness of the content available and its possible uses. Individual reporters and team leaders conduct ongoing conversations daily on enterprise work and the best ways to present it. The rules of engagement shared across platforms are a guide to identify the independence of each unit. These descriptions and distinction do

TABLE 5.6
The News Center Trends and Themes of Convergence

Creative	Technology	Individual Perspective	Organizational Perspective
Branding	BudgetBank software	Training	Good journalism
Advertising	Digital cell phones	Sharing information	Joint meetings
Enterprise projects	Digital video	Compensation	Multimedia
	Laptops	Layering the news	Collaboration
			First printing press for print, broad cast, and online

not eliminate blurred lines regarding editorial independence across platforms and raise questions regarding the diversity of voices and content received. The people at The News Center would argue that collaboration does not translate into capitulation. They work to be independent and develop content unique to their platform while keeping convergence at the forefront of expanding the journalism they practice.

REFERENCES

Carr, F. (2002a). The truth about convergence. Retrieved July 21, 2002, from http://www.poynter.org

Carr, F. (2002b). The Tampa model of convergence. Retrieved July 21, 2002, from http://www.poynter.org

Gordon, R. (2003). The meanings and implications of convergence. In K. Kawamoto (Ed.), *Digital journalism: Emerging media and the changing horizons of journalism* (pp. 57–73). Lanham, MD: Rowman & Littlefield.

Haas, T. (2000). Qualitative case study methods in newsroom research and reporting. In S. H. Iorio (Ed.), *Qualitative research in journalism: Taking it to the streets* (pp. 59–73). Mahwah, NJ: Lawrence Erlbaum Associates.

Media General. (2001). 2001 annual report. Retrieved April 16, 2004, from http://www.mediageneral.com

Media General. (2002). 2002 annual report. Retrieved April 16, 2004, from http://www.mediageneral.com

Media General. (2003). 2003 annual report. Retrieved April 16, 2004, from http://www.mediageneral.com

Rogers, E. M. (1995). Diffusion of innovations (4th ed.). New York: The Free Press.

Tampa Tribune Redesign: Collaborative Story Planning, Readers and You. (n.d.). *The Tampa Tribune*, Tampa, Florida.

The News Center Pledge. (n.d.). *The Tampa Tribune*, WFLA-TV News Channel 8, and TBO.com. The News Center, Tampa, Florida.

Thelen, G. (2002). Convergence is coming: Future newsrooms will require specialists who can learn to adapt. *Quill, 90*(6), 16.

Thelen, G. (2003, October 12). Dear Tribune readers: A commitment to you. *The Tampa Tribune*, p. A1.

6

Belo Corporation:
Market Dominance in Dallas

The tale of the castle moat in Dallas is different from the one found in most story books. This moat is figurative, not literal, and denotes a driveway through the center of the campus of Belo Corporation's Dallas properties. The entrance driveway separates the buildings for *The Dallas Morning News*, WFAA-TV, the ABC affiliate, TXCN statewide cable, and the offices of Belo Interactive Dallas Web sites properties. All of these entities are owned by Belo, but until 1997 were competitive and operated as if their sister properties were the enemy—thus, the entrance driveway served as the castle moat. A meeting called by Belo corporate executives in 1997 pulled up the drawbridge and dictated that convergence is the way in which the organization would conduct business (Murphy, 2002). The new mandate called for changes that included sharing resources, back-office consolidations, and promotion of group advertising and sales programs. Stuart Wilk, vice president and managing editor of *The Dallas Morning News*, recalled that WFAA-TV has always been a serious competitor for the newspaper over the years, and the parties had to work at changing the relationship (cited in Murphy, 2002). For Wilk, it was logical that the staff would inquire about the motives for integrating content across the business units. The rationale for change has ranged from economies of scale, saving money, sharing resources, and extending the brand. However, from Wilk's perspective, the answer that resonates for the staff is creating better journalism (cited in Murphy, 2002). Convergence in Dallas has gone through various phases, but the practice of converging content and resources across the business units is in full force.

MARKET DOMINANCE

Belo's Dallas properties were chosen for this case study because the company has experienced local media market dominance for several years and that position was enhanced when *The Dallas Herald* folded in 1991. The company is a convergence pioneer based on its efforts to use its multitude of resources, embrace new technologies, and expand its role in the Dallas market, where it is the premier media provider. In addition to *The Dallas Morning News*, WFAA, and TXCN cable, dallasnews.com was launched in 1996 as the electronic companion to the newspaper. Dallas Web sites for the TV and cable units joined this configuration of print, broadcast, and online presentation of content. From a staff of three, the online initiative has grown into Belo Interactive Dallas Web sites, which has a staff of about 37 people, and Al Dia's Spanish language Web site, whose staff of 2 serves 11 Dallas Web properties. The Dallas media properties are a laboratory for convergence because the previously disparate business units are working daily to integrate resources and content. The company blends the efforts of its media properties in Dallas to take advantage of cross-ownership of media in a major market. The analytical approach for each of the case studies in chapters 4, 5, and 6 is explanation building, an inductive approach that uses the collected data to build an explanation about the case (Haas, 2000). The purpose is to create a narrative to tell a story of how Belo's Dallas business units are using convergence as both a concept and process. Through a series of in-depth interviews, participant observation, and review of internal documents from 2002 to 2004, a snapshot is developed of the convergence process. This case study explicates specific elements of Belo's operations in Dallas to document examples of efforts to move convergence forward by utilizing resources across business units. Belo's Dallas properties were grandfathered into the 1975 Federal Communications Commission cross-ownership act because the properties were owned before the rule was enacted. Belo has taken advantage of the opportunity to hold a bounty of successful media properties in the same market. The FCC attempts in 2003 to lift the cross-ownership ban were overruled the following year by a federal court in Philadelphia. Belo continues to move forward and anticipates enhancing the convergence process in other markets at the future of cross-ownership unfolds in the courts. Table 6.1 is a compilation of Belo's Television Group, Newspaper Group, Cable News, and Belo Interactive properties collected from the corporate Web site and *Columbia Journalism Review*.

TABLE 6.1
Belo Corp.

Publishing and Newspapers

> The Dallas Morning News, Denton Record Chronicle, Al Dia (Dallas), Quick, Texas Almanac; The Providence Journal; Rhode Island Monthly; The Press-Enterprise, The Business Press, La Prensa, The Different Desert Daily (all Riverside, CA)

Television

> WFAA-TV, Dallas; KHOU-TV, Houston; KENS-TV, San Antonio; KBEJ-TV, San Antonio; KVUE-TV, Austin; KTVK-TV, Phoenix; KASW-TV, Phoenix; KMSB-TV, Tucson; KTTU-TV, Tucson; KING-TV, Seattle; KONG-TV, Seattle; KREM-TV, Spokane; KSKN-TV, Spokane; KTVB-TV, Boise; KGW-TV, Portland; KMOV-TV, St. Louis; WCNC-TV, Charlotte; WVEC-TV, Hampton; WWL-TV, New Orleans; WHAS-TV, Louisville

Cable

> Texas Cable News (TXCN); Northwest Cable News; Arizona News Channel; ¡Más! Arizona; Local News on Cable, Virginia; NewsWatch on Channel 15, Louisiana; 24 7 News Channel, Boise, Idaho

Interactive

> More than 30 Web sites, including the premium paid site Cowboysplus.com, several interactive alliances, and a broad range of Internet-based products

Other

> Dallas Mavericks (12.4% of the NBA franchise)

BELO INTERACTIVE DALLAS

Chris Kelley, editor of Belo Interactive Dallas Web sites, put it succinctly when he stated that the media industry is in a "digital renaissance" powered by the convergence of different content delivery technologies. "We are at the beginning of a digital renaissance, that is my term for it now, that in my view is a historic change, a once in history kind of change. It has affected all industry" (C. Kelley, personal communication, July 22, 2002). For example, Kelley told the story of a friend in the software business who was doing well, but later came to him to ask about obtaining employment with Belo. Kelley inquired about the software business, and the friend responded that the Internet had taken a bite out of his travel industry software business because people go directly to online travel companies such as Priceline or Expedia for travel services. "This is just within five years. So this renaissance is affecting our business. If you go to readership.org and look at readership patterns for age 30 and under, it is nightmarish for the newspaper industry" (C. Kelley, personal communication, July 22, 2002). Belo seeks to extend its brand of journalism across business units and works to capitalize on technological and other changes through convergence. "We try to extend the brand of journalism, *The Dallas Morning News* brand of journalism, dallasnews.com, WFAA Channel 8 quality to the web site, Texas Cable News to that statewide (audience). GuideLive.com continues to have our number one usability satisfaction. Our users like using it the most. I think because they can search and find what they want quickly" (C. Kelley, personal communication, July 22, 2002). Kelley is determined that Belo Interactive Dallas should build on these strengths as they move forward; from 1996 to 2004, the company saw a 20% to 40% revenue growth to about $30 million in operations. Belo is challenged to reach $100 million by 2010, according to Kelley (personal communication, April 29, 2004).

In August 2001, Belo Interactive consolidated the separate staffs of Dallasnews.com, TXCN.com, WFAA.com, and Guide Live.com, an entertainment site, into one staff to serve all the Web sites. The group is housed on the second floor of the newspaper building. There were gains and losses in the process, which included some jobs.

> The belief being that by consolidating these four independent staffs into one super staff to serve those four staffs would achieve a number of objectives. Once we converged the operations, it only made sense because we had duplicate functions underway at those sites. We eliminate duplication. We can right side the organization in the sense that while we lost 14 positions, most of which were vacant, we were able to essentially do a functional reorganization which allowed us to really put people where it made sense. (C. Kelley, personal communication, July 22, 2002)

The mission is breaking news and information Web sites. Once consolidation of the Web sites occurred, the company was better suited to achieve these objectives. Kelley stated the interactive sites are the only fully converged units. Belo Interactive Dallas' 11 Web sites include dallasnews.com, wfaa.com, txcn.com, dentonrc.com, aldiatx.com, guidelive.com, cowboysplus.com, texasalmanac.com, discoverdfw.com, bigtex.com, and community.dallasnews.com. The staff is responsible for original content, interactive features, and repurposing content from offline properties for the Web.

As editor for Belo Interactive Dallas Web sites, Kelley leads the operation with a 2004 organization chart identifying senior editors for News, Sports, Interactive, GuideLive/Lifestyles, and Strategic Development. Each is responsible for a team of editors, producers and application specialists for generating content for the Web sites. Kelley used a metaphor to describe the organization of the Interactive group in Dallas.

> When the Olympic flag is brought into the stadium everybody has a corner and if somebody drops a corner it looks really bad. They are all integrated. They all march together. They all have the same common objective. And that's the way I have set this operation up where each of the senior editors, while they have certain responsibilities for the site, they have functional responsibilities as well. And they all have to meet and talk and work together or somebody is going to drop a corner of the flag. (C. Kelley, personal communication, July 22, 2002)

To avoid the edges of the flag going down, communication and cooperation, two of the Seven Observations of Convergence discussed in chapter 1, are applicable. The Interactive editors must work together and with other business units to successfully move through the convergence process and select the most suitable content for integration. An early challenge for the converged units was managing the different information technology platforms. In 2002, Dallasnews.com was using a web publishing system called VelocIT to interface with the newspaper publishing system called CCI, which is a pagination system. The TV station has a system called INews, and TXCN uses its own system. Kelley said the challenge was to get all the systems talking and finding ways to grab information quickly. Web sites require a great deal of programming and frequent checks to ensure that they run smoothly. Kelley stated that Web software serves advertising content needs differently than content for news, so the interactive team has worked through numerous components over the years and improved operations.

COWBOYSPLUS.COM

Belo Interactive's premium, paid Web site CowboysPlus.com (see Fig. 6.1) debuted in August 2003. The site incorporates coverage from *The Dallas Morning News*, dallasnews.com, WFAA-TV, and Texas Cable News for comprehensive Dallas Cowboys coverage. Subscriptions for the debut were listed at $29.95 a year, $19.95 for 6 months, and a monthly rate of $9.95 (Carlton, 2003). A week after its launch, the site had about 1,500 subscribers, and by April 2004 had about 3,000 subscribers, according to Kelley (personal interview, April 29, 2004). The site continues to explore the possibilities for Cowboys fans and aficionados that are drawn to any information about the NFL team. Features of the premium pay site include a full-time reporter, e-mail alerts, exclusive columns, video of historic moments, and game stories from the newspaper since 1960. The pay site was pondered for about 2 years and reflected efforts to respond to other sites targeting fans of NFL teams. CowboysPlus.com is reflective of industry efforts to market premium content for pay, which has been mostly led by *The Wall Street Journal*. Other media such as the *Pittsburgh Post-Gazette* and the *Milwaukee Jour-*

FIG. 6.1.   A screen shot of CowboysPlus.com. Reprinted with permission by Belo Interactive Dallas.

nal have also used pay sites to expand coverage of NFL teams (Carlton, 2003).

QUICK

Also launched in 2003 was *Quick*, a color tabloid targeted to 18- to 34-year-olds in Dallas. The free weekly is published Monday through Friday and is distributed in 3,600 locations in the Dallas/Ft. Worth area. The quick, short stories, photos, graphics, and celebrity gossip are meant to grab young professionals who are on the go, but want to keep abreast of the news, what to do, and where to go. The tabloid covers local happenings and hot spots, and includes short items on U.S. and world news, sports, and business. Features include the Day Tripper, a must-do list; and The Ten, a list of the top 10 stories of the day. The Web site quickfw.com was added in September 2004 to complement the tabloid and keep the targeted group in touch with the world around them. "The website will enhance the Quick print product by offering more extensive, searchable entertainment listings, unique lifestyle content and up-to-the-minute news," a company news release stated (Quick Launches, 2004). *Quick*, a product of *The Dallas Morning News* and quickdfw.com, was developed by Kelley and editors and producers at the Belo Interactive sites.

MEDIA PRODUCTS

Kelley also pointed to additional products that the Belo Interactive Dallas group developed that have created additional revenue for the company. By repacking and repurposing content such as DVDs, CDs, and other products, the group created an additional revenue stream. Information was repackaged for sale in tangible forms useful to the audience. For example, there is a CD of the *2003 State Fair of Texas Cookbook*, a CD of *Tragedy over Texas: The Columbia Shuttle Disaster*, or a 40th anniversary collector's edition DVD of *The Story Behind the Story: JFK Dallas, November 22, 1963* (see Figs. 6.4 and 6.5). Each of these media products, produced by the interactive staff in Dallas, brought in additional revenue for the division. In 2003, the success of the sale of the products translated into bonuses for the staff who experienced an additional payoff for their creativity, according to Kelley (personal communication, April 29, 2004). As convergence emerges, companies will continue to seek ways for the online divisions to generate profits, and these types of products appear to be a feasible venue. There will also be a migration from registration-only sites to paid-subscription sites such as *The Wall Street Journal.* The media industry's future may include convergence, but it includes the convergence process at a cost that content providers online will eventually try to get their audience to share the cost.

WEB STYLE GUIDE

Kelley's team has solidified the importance of the Belo Interactive group's professionalism, ethics, and integrity through the development of the *Dallas Web Sites Style and Operations Guide* (Fig. 6.2 lists the Web sites in the guide). This online style guide is significant for a number of reasons. First, it created a bound notebook that serves as a document for consistency across Web sites. It is a procedural manual with guidelines, forms, and details of specific processes. The internal document, *Dallas Web Sites Mission: First, Informed, and Interactive* (see Fig. 6.3), is indicative of the accomplishments the company seeks by using the guidebook.

The style guide focuses on operations and responsibilities. For example, the senior editors are responsible for managing their designated areas, and the specific requirements of staff to disseminate content are addressed. What makes this style guide unique is that it customizes the needs for multimedia for Belo Web sites. The procedures for use of audio, banners, FLASH presentations, PDFs, photography, and graphics are spelled out in detail. For example, FLASH should be used if the story being told would benefit from animation, sound, or interactivity. If these three elements are not used, then HTML should be the process for uploading the content to the Web, according to the stylebook. Kelley described the stylebook as a unifier that helps minimize missteps and better serve the audience. The stylebook describes the method to coordinate with the other business units when exchanging content.

Belo Interactive

D A L L A S

dallasnews.com

wfaa.com

txcn.com

dentonrc.com

aldiatx.com

guidlive.com

cowboysplus.com

texasalmanac.com

discoverdfw.com

bigtex.com

community.dallasnews.com

FIG. 6.2.   Printed with permission by Belo Interactive Dallas.

Dallas Web Sites Mission
First, informed and interactive

dallasnews.com

wfaa.com

txcn.com

guidelive.com

aldiatx.com

dentonrc.com

quickdfw.com

cowboysplus.com

texasalmanac.com

discoverdfw.com

bigtex.com

community.dallasnews.com

First:
We urgently connect users/readers/viewers to information that they don't know about.

Informed:
We anticipate users' needs and make them smarter for having spent time with us.

Interactive:
We connect psychologically and emotionally with our audiences.

1. Our journalism is memorable—strong visuals, smart headlines and reader-focused content. We tell readers why they should care and, in turn, we ask them to weigh in with their views, share their experiences and help us tell the story when appropriate.

2. Breaking news is what we do best. In 2004, New This Hour will expand to include several breaking/new stories each hour. People are in a hurry, so shorter is better. We will send out more breaking news alerts in 2004.

3. Sports is the No. 1 interest of our users/readers/viewers, and we play sports appropriately and deploy our interactive resources accordingly.

4. Our Top Story is the talker of the day. We decide the night before or very early in the day what the story will be and layer it appropriately with video, graphics and interactive questions.

5. We leverage the best of our own content on all Dallas sites and across the BI network as appropriate. We leverage the best of our offline partners' content.

6. We program our sites to day parts—morning, noon and night, weekends and holidays. And we go out of our way to help users find news and information on our sites.

7. People need a break from the serious. We offer them many choices.

8. Our multimedia story-telling is world-class.

9. Our design and visuals are award-winning.

10. Our programming and special projects are state-of-the art. Our Web sites' operations are the most efficient and effective anywhere.

FIG. 6.3. Printed with permission by Belo Interactive Dallas.

FIG. 6.4. Printed with permission by Belo Interactive Dallas.

FIG. 6.5.　Printed with permission by Belo Interactive Dallas.

DAILY CONVERGENCE PRACTICES

The staff of each business unit in Dallas has routines that occur daily in the process of gathering and disseminating content. The convergence process is incorporated through resources, daily meetings, and communication among the staff. A typical day begins with a 9 a.m. WFAA-TV news meeting where early assignments and items for the day are discussed. Oscar Martinez, senior editor for interactive, in charge of multimedia coordination, attends the TV station meeting to share and identify possible convergence opportunities. Belo Interactive group holds a news meeting at 10 a.m. to discuss what is on the Web sites and other plans for the day. At 10:45 a.m., *The Dallas Morning News* editorial budget meeting begins, where there is more discussion of what is on the agenda across the units. Kelley said the Belo Interactive group also has a place at the table during the 3:00 p.m. *Dallas Morning News* page one meeting run by the managing editor. At that meeting, a group of editors surround the conference room table and fill chairs along the walls. The lights are dim and an editor/producer from the Web site sits at a laptop and clicks on pages of Dallasnews.com to reveal what the Web site has posted as newspaper editors discuss story offerings. The print editors must consider what they will do differently for the newspaper than was viewed on the screen. Kelley said it has focused editors on the mission they call "U2—Unique and Unduplicated content" for the newspaper (personal communication, July 22, 2002). This pushes everyone to be creative and think more strategically about what content is offered and how it is presented.

WFAA-TV

The Web sites have also gained currency by placing an assistant editor in the WFAA-TV newsroom on the overnight 11 p.m. to 7 a.m. shift. The overnight editor is constantly updating and collecting information for *The Dallas Morning News*, WFAA-TV, TXCN cable, and Belo Interactive sites. By 2004, Walt Zwirko, a 20-year broadcast veteran, worked the overnight assignment desk at the TV station, monitoring scanners and updating the Web site (personal communication, April 29, 2004). Zwirko, who joined wfaa.com in 1995, makes calls on stories or dispatches photographers for the TV or newspaper in the event of breaking news. Of the array of equipment at Zwirko's disposal, his use of a TiVo digital recording device increases the ability to grab still frames for the Internet or video. The editor's presence at the TV station overnight has allowed a jump start on breaking news and events. There is also a Web reporter in the newspaper newsroom on the early morning shift for the same reasons, reporting and gathering information that can appear on the Web site early in the morning. For convergence, these efforts keep the Web site current and connected to coverage from the different platforms.

Another take on convergence comes from top management at WFAA-TV. "I read a lot about convergence. And I don't think anybody does it better than Belo does in this market," said David Duitch, vice president news for WFAA-TV (personal communication, July 24, 2002). "I really don't. You have got your Chicago experience and Tampa, but I think it's done right here." For Duitch, the convergence process among the Belo business units has evolved into a mutually beneficial arrangement for all parties. When asked to discuss some of the observations of convergence listed in chapter 1—culture, communication, compensation, and commitment—Duitch contended the cultural shift has been conducive to change.

> The first C is culture, but not because broadcasting is different from print, although it certainly is. But that at least in this situation, you have a very long history of people in this newsroom, WFAA, wanting to absolutely annihilate any other media competitor to be first on the scene and to be the first to report a story. Not only the other TV stations but *The Dallas Morning News*. You have people at *The Dallas Morning News* who want to do the same thing, and being jointly owned you had a company across the street, I mean literally across the street, that said "thou should not talk to the other property." We have government rules that don't allow it, you can't do it. So you have this alley, this driveway, that really was a raging river that no one tried to cross and then suddenly the waters were parted and we were told it was okay to talk and there was great trepidation. (D. Duitch, personal communication, July 24, 2002)

From Duitch's perspective, although corporate executives brought everyone together in 1997, convergence in Dallas actually got underway in 1999 and it was an uphill sell. There were staffers who felt, "I still want to beat them." Duitch responded that they do so by getting an idea for a story at WFAA before *The Dallas Morning News*, but if the decision is to go with a story, they tell the other business units. The same occurs on the print side, and the culture changes to sharing information and resources.

Communication is essential because all of the parties involved have to talk and understand what is trying to be accomplished by each business unit in Dallas, individually and together as converged partners. Duitch added:

> Communication is critical and it starts in this scenario, it started at the top and it is gradually pushing its way down. But first it was presidents of each company talking to each other, then it was vice presidents talking to each other and then managing editors talking to each other and then now it is at a point where you have reporters talking to each other, which is the best form of convergence you can have. (personal communication, July 24, 2002)

Duitch has watched Belo evolve over the past years to a point where content is shared from the weather pages to promoting *The Dallas Morning News* business stories on TV for the following day.

> But it is much deeper than that. We have reporters who cover stories and then write them for *The Dallas Morning News* and *The Dallas Morning News* has a reporter who writes for the newspaper and then produces television stories for us. We have people who as part of their daily checklist of what they have to do, talk to my counterpoint at *The Dallas Morning News*. So I would say the communication is key and we have got it to a point where it works. (D. Duitch personal communication, July 24, 2002)

A joint Web process has developed in which TXCN cable, Belo Interactive, *The Dallas Morning News*, and WFAA exchange news tips via e-mail in the afternoon. This online process keeps all parties abreast of the information being developed for distribution.

The convergence system works at Belo and continues to move forward in useful ways, according to Duitch. The compensation issue is still unclear in Dallas as well as at other companies that practice convergence. In Chicago and Tampa, performance reviews may address someone's efforts to include multimedia into their work. Yet there are no specific management directives that state what scenarios would dictate additional pay for being part of the convergence process. Duitch admitted that reporters are asked to do more than, perhaps, 5 years ago:

> Are we asking them to, okay, I want you to cover the city council meeting for broadcasting, and I want you to cover the football game for the newspaper, and I want you to cover the fashion show for the Internet—no. But, if you are at the city council meeting, and you are covering the city council meeting, write it for broadcast, and if you can, write something for the web. (personal communication, July 24, 2002)

During a 2002 interview, however, Duitch added that reporters were not asked to dramatically shift gears to cover a different story in the course of a day for one of the media partners. The question remains where the changes in skills and responsibilities will translate into additional compensation.

The commitment to convergence is evidenced at Belo by the potential to enhance the product and share resources. Again Duitch used the staff at WFAA-TV to illustrate. He has 20 reporters, but on any given day only six to eight reporters may be on the street due to vacations, health, or work on long-term projects. Meanwhile *The Dallas Morning News* has 300-plus reporters as resources to share information. Duitch stated,

> I've got a company that will give me journalists working on my website, so that it can be competitive and up to date, and better than any other TV station website in my market. Why wouldn't I welcome that opportunity? And if I can get expanded time for a story on my cable channel, and get statewide distribution to boot, why wouldn't I want to go over there for their extended coverage? It only makes sense. (personal communication, July 24, 2002)

The convergence process has expanded to include a non-Belo entity—WBAP radio in the Dallas market. According to Duitch, the radio station has partnered with Belo: They have access to everything WBAP airs, and the radio station gets access to everything WFAA airs. The impact of the Web relationship with other Belo partners is evident through new channels of activity. If the TV station wants to know what viewers think about a story, a chat room can be set up on wfaa.com to allow the viewers to talk.

> I mean the opportunities are enormous and any news organization that says, you know, I am just broadcast, or I am just print, they are absolutely burying their head in the sand and they are not going to survive in the future. (D. Duitch, personal communication, July 24, 2002)

Convergence has transformed operations across business units in Dallas. In 2004, Duitch was named Vice President/Capital Bureau and will carry his convergence perspective to Belo's Washington, DC, bureau in 2005, where he joins the integrated staff of TV and newspaper operations.

TEXAS CABLE NEWS (TXCN)

In Texas, Belo executives enacted numerous strategic changes for the organization, particularly in the Dallas market, to be the most effective for the business and environment—whether it was cross-ownership of media properties, starting TXCN statewide cable, or moving to convergence as a business practice across platforms in 1997. The story of the driveway moat discussed at the beginning of this chapter is part of that change. Steve Ackerman, executive news director of TXCN, recalls long-time Belo staffers sharing what they called "the moat speech" (personal communication, July 26, 2002).

According to Ackerman, the culture inherited in Dallas was primarily governed by regulation. Belo's properties in Dallas were one of the legal duopoly markets, as in Chicago. The federal government made it clear that if Belo wanted to own WFAA-TV and *The Dallas Morning News*, the company had to agree to maintain them as totally separate organizations. Belo took the edict seriously. There are staffers who remember a meeting with the CEO in which they were told the driveway between the business units was a moat, and nothing was to cross that moat. "The only exception to that moat rule was that employees of WFAA were allowed to go into the *Morning News* building for two reasons. They could go to the cafeteria to eat, and they could go to the nurse if they were hurt. That was it" (S. Ackerman, personal communication, July 26, 2002).

The TV and newspaper were competitors, and staying apart was imperative. From Ackerman's vantage point, this was good for Belo because executives felt that if any overzealous congressman visited Dallas in search of a violation, the moat and competitiveness demonstrated they were separate business units. By 1998, when Belo decided to start Texas Cable News, Ackerman had joined the scene. Ackerman was told he would get a facility, which was down the driveway and behind the newspaper building. However, he would have to use content that was already produced by other Belo broadcast units. Ackerman would be repurposing content on the cable station and would not get new reporters. Belo owns not only WFAA, but stations in Houston and San Antonio to supply content to TXCN. That is the culture that Ackerman entered, and he started operations at the cable station under that premise. As he traveled to meetings at WFAA-TV and then crossed the driveway to attend an afternoon page one meeting at the newspaper, his actions set a precedent because of the ingrained culture, according to Ackerman. The cable station launched in December 1998 and by 1999 was on the air and slowly starting to build its presence. "We were like a little tot, but we [could] walk several steps" (S. Ackerman, personal communication, July 26, 2002).

THE STORY OF THE EMUS

There is a learning curve for convergence, and every organization perhaps has an epiphany that shapes how it views content sharing. In Dallas, the story of the emus illustrates how the Belo Dallas properties worked through the issue of precedent for presenting a story across platforms. Emus are large, flightless Australian birds similar to the ostrich. In the late 1990s, some enterprising entrepreneurs decided to raise emus in Dallas. There was not a lot of money to be made raising emus, so some owners abandoned the birds. Ackerman received a call one afternoon from the newspaper coordinator that someone had given a videotape to a reporter regarding mistreatment of the birds, many of which had been abandoned and destroyed in an area south of Dallas.

Ackerman entered the fray when the cable station was asked to dub the tape so that frames could be pulled for use in the newspaper. Of course Ackerman wanted to use some of the video, but he was informed that it was a *Morning News* exclusive. Ackerman could not use the video until the 10:00 p.m. broadcast, and he could not share the information with WFAA-TV. "There was already a bridge across the moat, the moat was gone. It was a footbridge, and it is still a little shaky" (S. Ackerman, personal communication, July 26, 2002). He lost the argument to run the tape on cable or share it with WFAA, and at about 6 p.m. that day, the story appeared on the TV station of a local competitor. Ackerman called the news director at WFAA to confirm that he saw the competitor's story, informing him that he had the tape, but could not use it because it was an exclusive for the newspaper. Ackerman tags this as a breakthrough moment for sharing content across the business units. Belo managers were forced to realize the need to identify who really was their competitor. Although the *Morning News* did not want the newspaper in Fort Worth to get the story, they missed that other TV stations in the Dallas market might have the same video. Another TV station had the tape and ran it before Belo. Whistleblowers like convergence are platform agnostic—they just want to get the information out as soon as possible.

Lessons were learned from the emu incident. At TXCN cable, which is primarily a repurposing operation and does not generate a great deal of original material, breaking news gets on any platform as quickly as it can be placed there. According to Ackerman, as a practical matter, this approach with breaking news permeates all of the business units. The information is distributed as soon as possible. Enterprise stories, however, belong to the origi-

nating organization. "There are two key words in that phrase—
'belong'—there is ownership—and 'organization'—it doesn't belong to the reporter, it belongs to the organization," Ackerman
stated. If a manager considers a story enterprise, all she has to say
is, "It's ours, and then we all stand back" (S. Ackerman, personal
communication, July 26, 2002). Senior managers are open to discuss if they want to use an enterprise story in a different manner,
but protocol goes to the originator.

Ackerman contended this is the way content sharing should
be—owned by the organization and not editors, reporters, or any
individual. He suggested the economic benefits of convergence are
easy to see from things such as shared editorial content. In political
coverage, for example, the cable station benefits from an experienced political newspaper reporter joining a similar colleague from
the TV station on a cable show to provide insight on politics. Belo
could collaborate with other entities to produce debates on local
and statewide political races to air on cable. However, the benefit of
convergence for the audience—viewer, user, or reader—and all of
those terms used at the Dallas properties is not readily clear. For
example, the newspaper develops different types of content for the
newspaper. The cable station may try to capture some of this material by inviting the House and Garden section editor to come and
talk each week on a cable show. On air, it may appear as if cable is
promoting a newspaper section.

> From the viewer concept of things, I think sometimes we talk about
> convergence and we don't stop and think about what benefit it brings
> the viewer. In the area of political coverage, it's obvious. It gives us
> clout, it gives us insight. I get it. In some of these other areas we are
> still trying to figure it out. (S. Ackerman, personal communication,
> July 26, 2002)

From a business perspective on convergence, there are back office functions that can be more efficient, such as human resources
or accounting. "Whether they really are more efficient are not, we
can argue about that, but generally speaking we know what that is.
From the selling viewpoint, can we really sell more ad time, more ad

space together? I don't know. I think the jury is still out on that one" (S. Ackerman, personal communication, July 26, 2002). Over the past 3 years, Belo and other convergence pioneers discussed in this book have reported incremental revenue gains in advertising and from online operations through cross-promotions, multimedia ad packages, and other products. So whether from best practices observations of culture, collaboration, compensation, or competition, the best model for convergence is still evolving.

Ackerman contended that critics as well as proponents of convergence need to be aware that we are in a world where everybody's margins are being sliced thinner. The economic issue of convergence operations prompted Ackerman to recall the words of a general manager, for whom he worked 20 years earlier, regarding a technology device that his TV station was considering at that time:

> There is a little bit of money to be made in this and a lot of people who want to share it.... That is one of the pitfalls from a business standpoint that we just have to be alert to. And we are an example of that. There is money to be made in a 24 hour cable channel. People want to be able to watch news 24 hours a day. They want to see something with a little more focus from a Texas point of view. The problem is that the cable operator wants to make money, we want to make money. The journalist who contributes to what we do wants to make money. Everybody wants to make money off of it and we keep slicing the ham thinner and thinner. This is a thin slice of ham. (S. Ackerman, personal communication, July 26, 2002)

Ackerman's metaphor is illustrative of the manner in which members of an organization from top to bottom view the economic components of convergence through different lenses.

PERSPECTIVES ON THE CONVERGENCE PROCESS

The convergence process takes on different meanings for individuals, from the editors and reporters, to the graphic designers, photographers, and team members. In-depth interviews with various members of the staff and participant observation in the various newsrooms over a 3-year period revealed different perspectives on what everyone feels they do and how it integrates into the process. Belo Interactive extends its operations by using the staff in different ways to help facilitate integration. For example, the interactive unit staffs the overnight shift with one of its editors in the TV station newsroom. The editor's location at the TV station allows the person to keep abreast of breaking news, dispatch photographers for the TV station or newspaper if necessary, and make calls on news stories. According to Chris Kelley, because the interactive unit has someone posted in the TV station, it builds relationships for convergence across business units and has allowed the Web site to get a jump start on numerous stories.

Another insider approach for the interactive group is to have a reporter at the newspaper. Kimberly Durnan is a reporter for Belo Interactive Dallas Web sites. She works the early morning shift starting at 6 a.m. in the newsroom of *The Dallas Morning News*. Her shift dovetails with the overnight reporter for the interactive group, who works until 7 a.m. in the WFAA-TV newsroom. Durnan is a former Associated Press (AP) reporter with a traditional print background, but her move into interactive has been a fruitful one. As an AP reporter, she was accustomed to the constant updating of information at the news service and the need to cull radio and TV stations.

A typical day starts with Durnan picking up night notes from Metro reporters and their editors. Because there is someone listening to scanners overnight, she gleans information from that source. She checks through the information and makes calls and updates where necessary so the Web site starts off the day with the most recent information. Belo Interactive is aware that most of its Web site traffic occurs during the work day when people arrive to work and log on, "So we try to get stuff really cooking and going before that traffic comes unto the website. They will have something that is not in the newspaper that is a little fresher and updated for them to read" (K. Durnan, personal communication, July 22, 2004). Durnan's reporting includes collecting information by phone in the office or going to the scene on certain breaking news. Collaboration is essential for convergence to be successful. Durnan gets several stories in process and updated so that as the newspaper staff arrive later in the morning, they get a head start on the material they will finish building for the next day's paper.

Convergence includes cultural change, and Durnan is aware of several ways she currently works that are different from print-only positions she held in the past, which included work in the Rio Grande Valley and Des Moines, Iowa, and at the *Fort-Worth Star Telegram*. In addition to reporting and writing, Durnan now carries a digital camera when she goes out to cover a story. "I ... shoot photos with it. I was a little worried about it at first I guess, and I took a class.... But, it is kind of different on the web because it is more like a poster, and it is not like I have to compete with photographers" (K. Durnan, personal communication, July 22, 2002). Durnan views her carrying the digital camera as a way to quickly obtain photos that can be transmitted by laptop. Photographers have numerous assignments, and they can move forward while reporters such as Durnan may get quick and convenient shots for immediate use because she was accessible to the subject. Durnan finds other benefits that extend across the business units. In one instance, an overnight reporter captured digital photos of a more than $40 million mansion in Dallas under construction that burned in 2002. The six to eight photos were overlapped and used for a panoramic FLASH presentation on the Web site, an online complement to the newspaper story.

Durnan notes that another change is the interactive aspect of her work as a reporter on the Web site. She gets a significant amount of e-mail that adds a dimension to stories that she might not otherwise obtain. For example, while covering a story of a tragic out-of-state car accident involving a local family, Durnan immediately began receiving e-mails from neighbors, coworkers, and friends of the family. She contacted several of the people and was able to provide rich detail for a story that started in an Arkansas traffic accident, but had great impact on the audience for the Web site. Durnan said she was also able to stay in touch with some of the contacts to present a better story on the family and the tragic loss for people who knew them. She said people were constantly e-mailing her, so it turned into an interactive experience building the story.

Although Durnan had not foreseen working as a journalist with Belo Interactive, she reiterates that it was compatible with her previous experience. Also she has found some professional growth through experiences using digital cameras or interacting with sources by e-mail working on a story. She receives a few complaints, but it is usually about matters beyond her control, such as subliminal advertising appearing on a Web story. Durnan predicts convergence as a process will continue to move forward and perhaps become more competitive in the future. She suggests that, as more people log on and use their computers for different types of activities, media companies will push to tap into those uses. Durnan believes that AP and others will become more competitive and use digital audio, video, and packages like Belo Interactive's converged operations to reach audiences. Tom Curley, president and CEO of AP, at the Online News Association's 2004 convention echoed similar predictions for AP work, new media devices, and new software applications and their impact on the convergence process (cited in Finberg, 2004).

Ellen Henderson, senior editor for GuideLive/Lifestyles, can attest to the changes that have occurred with online content delivery (personal communication, July 22, 2002). She is also responsible for the entertainment sections of dallasnews.com and wfaa.com content that might complement or develop originally for the Web. Henderson became editor of the section in 2000 during what she termed a *honeymoon period* for the Web. In Dallas and across the country, media outlets were experimenting with what worked on the Web. Henderson recalls a large staff with numerous freelancers entering data and producing content. Then the dot.com bust hit in 2001, and online operations were streamlined by staff and resources. "I sort of guided this ship through some lean times. Right now we are doing pretty well, because of that but also because we learned more and more what our audiences wanted" (E. Henderson, personal communication, July 22, 2002).

For example, GuideLive.com considered several approaches to content—from coffee shops to guitar playing and restaurant and movie reviews. It was later learned that it was better to provide the content online that was most popular and useful to the audience. At GuideLive.com, the terms *usability* and *functional-ity* started to resonate.

> What we found was we got the most return on our work from the ar-
> eas that were really popular. Movie reviews, restaurant reviews ... the
> big shows, music concerts. We were not getting anybody looking at
> those coffee shops [and] guitars, so why were we bothering? I think
> our mission has really changed. Not that we have everything that has
> ever been done. But we will always have something for you to do. (E.
> Henderson, personal communication, July 22, 2002)

The content and organization of GuideLive.com has evolved over the years. GuideLive was launched in 1998 as Microsoft Sidewalk and CitySearch portals were being used across the country to provide city guides. Belo, as an established media source, wanted to provide this type of information in the Dallas/Ft. Worth area. Henderson stated that GuideLive started as a partnership with CitySearch and shared the use of its sophisticated database that was already set up and in use. She said it was a partnership in which CitySearch provided the technology and GuideLive provided the content. "You know, credible, trusted, comprehensive content from the staff over at the newspaper" (E. Henderson, personal communication, July 22, 2002). Sidewalk was eventually purchased by CitySearch. GuideLive underwent a redesign in 2002 and is a fully comprehensive entertainment site.

In 2004, Belo ended its contract with CitySearch for Web templates and brought the service inhouse. GuideLive content includes restaurant reviews, movie and concert reviews, and the top places to go in the area. Because the site is online, the usability and functionality of content are increased for the audience. "In general, we feel like the way we adapt [content] to the web is by putting it into the search engine. So that instead of just turning the pages to whatever you want, you can search for an event anyway you want" (E. Henderson, personal communication, July 22, 2002). It provides a different dimension for use of the information found on the site. For example, in the newspaper Guide section, there might be pages of agate type of restaurant reviews and listings. On GuideLive.com, users can type in the name of a restaurant, city, or cuisine for the full text of the original review, location and map, price range and hours, owners, and any recent changes at the restaurant. Does any of this raise the criticism that media outlets cannibalize their audiences and content from offline to online? For Henderson, this is not the case:

> We don't take anything away from Guide (the newspaper section). I think they do an amazing job. Everybody loves Guide.... One of the best, most popular products that the paper makes. And they do a great job in writing reviews. We also pull reviews from different zoned sections of the paper. The Plano zone, the Richardson zone; they each do their own reviews. We pull from that also. So we have the only place that has all those weekly reviews in one place. And we actually publish them early, which is one of the great things. Guide publishes reviews on Friday. We publish the reviews on Thursdays, so we get a little scoop on that. But you know we have archives for all those older reviews.... But for us to take that review that is so credible and so valuable and then add all of this extra stuff to, this really is the key that people come to our site for. This is the number one thing. (E. Henderson, personal communication, July 22, 2002)

Those extras have made GuideLive.com popular because of its functionality. People can choose and find the information they seek—from what to do to where the hot places are in the Dallas/Ft. Worth area. Complementing or producing original content separate from the newspaper product is a challenge for the online site. Henderson pointed out that the Guide staff prepares in terms of one week at a time, but Guidelive.com is online every day, 24 hours a day. Thus, the online staff must work to keep ahead of the game with its own scheduling, database work, longer pieces, calendar, and announcements.

Lessons vary about what translates online versus in print. An interesting piece from the Arts section of the newspaper may not resonate in the electronic environment. Also online chat rooms were used early on to explore interactivity on the site. Readers could chat with a reviewer from the newspaper, but the process did not catch on and people were not logging on for the chats. Henderson recalled once that coverage of the Cannes Film Festival was used online as well as in the newspaper. A correspondent in Cannes wrote good articles that were well received in print, but did not translate online. According to Henderson,

> The three things I felt I really learned was that people do not come to GuideLive, that site specifically to read, or to build community, or to hang around. They are not in the mood. I don't think the site evokes that kind of thing. They come for information, period. They want to find what they need. They want to get it and they want to get out again. That is the way they use. It is all about functionality. (personal communication, July 22, 2002)

However, content that was not successful on GuideLive.com would do well on dallasnews.com. Henderson suspected that people were expecting to find that type of information on the newspaper site.

The challenge is finding what content works best and where. For Henderson, GuideLive's strength is in the comprehensive coverage it provides on entertainment and activities in the area. The functionality of the site keeps people coming back at any time of day. Henderson contended that there is an advantage to having a separate staff for newspaper and online operations.

> I think there is a real benefit to having those of us over here who are just focused on the web.... The way I have been sort of researching the web, and not kind of caught up in the newspaper, but really forward thinking about what does it mean to be an online journalism site, and what are our readers expecting has proven beneficial. (personal communication, July 22, 2002)

These are the types of concerns that Henderson feels the interactive units can focus on when considering what makes good journalism to extend the brand online. The technology (e.g., page visits, IP addresses) allows the company to know about who is using what online, and decisions can be made to change from that point. Henderson explained how the Web affords more opportunity to know the audience and what they are doing. On the Web, one can learn what people are clicking on, which articles they are reading, which sections they visit most, or how many people visited a section. The wealth of information also includes more direct communication with readers because it is so easy for them to click for feedback through such vehicles as e-mail.

Belo Interactive started online registration in 2001 and can glean from that information the sites and stories that are being accessed. By 2002, Kelley said the network-wide registration was approximately 1.2 million, with dallasnews.com accounting for more than half of that number. The dallasnews.com registration is about 710,000 to 715,000 registered users. Kelley suggested that, although not an "apple to apple" comparison, *The Dallas Morning News* has a Monday through Saturday daily circulation of 511,000 and Sunday of about 825,000.

BUSINESS AND ECONOMICS

On January 1, 2001, Belo Corp. became the official name of the former A. H. Belo Corporation. The name change was a small part of the growing influence of the Dallas-based media company with publishing, broadcasting, and interactive business groups. Belo's properties are geographically clustered in Texas; the Southwest, Northwest, and Mid-Atlantic; and Rhode Island. This book focuses on Texas, specifically the media properties in the Dallas/Ft. Worth area. The two largest properties are *The Dallas Morning News* and WFAA-TV, although this case study examines four newspapers, one TV station, one cable, and 11 interactive outlets in the Dallas market area.

Table 6.2 shows revenue for the company over a 3-year period, during which there was modest growth since 2001 because of 9/11 and the recession in the economy. However, the interactive group demonstrated steady growth.

In 2001, revenues were just under $1.4 billion, and the company's 19 TV stations and 4 daily newspapers were faring well. Belo Interactive included 34 Web sites corporate-wide, with several interactive alliances and Internet-based products. The goal was to try and expand the interactive area with innovative services. Belo joined the CareerBuilder network, which offered online services to

TABLE 6.2
Belo Financials (in thousands)

Revenue	2003	2002	2001
Television Group	$ 646,666	$ 657,538	$ 597,881
Newspaper Group	745,941	733,631	737,594
Interactive Media	24,595	19,472	13,065
Other	18,809	17,266	16,163
Total revenue	$ 1,436,011	$ 1,427,907	$ 1,364,703

job seekers and employers on a local and national scale. Interactive revenues, however, were primarily from ads on the Web sites (Securities and Exchange Commission, 2001).

The 2002 annual report, *Working Together*, expounded on the theme of togetherness and integrations (Belo Corp., 2002). Cash flow improved in 2002, and revenue growth occurred in each quarter. The rhetoric of the annual report is to speak to shareholders, and the expectations are to make the prognosis sound favorable. The Television Group and Belo Interactive performance increased, whereas the Newspaper Group revenues decreased, with classified lineage down. In 2002, Belo celebrated its 160th anniversary as a business—the oldest in Texas.

Belo is proud of its efforts at making convergence a part of its business practices. The 2003 annual report stated, "Convergence is a given throughout Belo; it is built into the systems and processes of every newspaper, television station, cable news channel and website" (Belo Corp., 2003). This translates into using all available means to share content, resources, cross-promotion, and cross-branding. Belo Interactive showed a 26.3% revenue increase to $25 million in 2003—from $19 million in 2002.

Attention on the interactive area reflects an effort to show where multimedia and integration are making a difference for the organization. An internal brochure for Belo Interactive Dallas illustrates a different perspective on the impact of the unit. *The Dallas Morning News* launched dallasnews.com in 1996.

The Web site's role as an integral part of the company was evident when the newspaper scooped itself by publishing an exclusive story on dallasnews.com of Timothy McVeigh, the Oklahoma City bomber, before it was printed in the newspaper on February 28, 1997 (Belo Interactive Dallas, n.d.; Zavoina & Reichert, 2000). Belo's Dallas properties are converged operations that continue to deliver content on every platform using technology that keeps the organization connected.

SUMMARY

Convergence is a concept and process at Belo, and specifically in its Dallas market, as described in this case study. The members of the various business units actively use communication, collaboration, and a corporate commitment to keep sharing of resources and content on the front burner. There are common themes, trends, and concepts that can be gleaned from the in-depth interviews, observations, and documents collected for more than 3 years in Dallas. From an individual and organizational perspective, some issues stand out as important in the evolution of convergence in Dallas. Table 6.3 highlights components of convergence that are indicative of the operations in Dallas.

TABLE 6.3
Dallas Convergence Themes and Trends

Creative	Technology	Individual Perspective	Organizational Perspective
Cowboysplus.com	Online search capabilities	Training	Practice good journalism
Partnerships	Functionality	Cultural change	Readers and viewers/users
Special projects	Usability	Compensation	Trial and error with content
Online products			Collaboration
			Competition

The staff on every level and business unit in Dallas are tuned in to see where convergence will take the organization. For now the driveway moat is just well-worn pavement used by all parties. The sense of competition remains. Although breaking news moves forward immediately across platforms, enterprising stories offer each business unit an opportunity to bring forward different projects. The early culture at Belo's Dallas operations may have been competitive and desperate, but collaboration abounds. Not everyone has adapted, and cultural changes still exist for acceptance and a new way of doing business. A marketing video on the Belo corporate Web site in 2004, "A Day in the Life of Belo," demonstrates its philosophy on convergence, which includes enhancing and improving revenues, efficiencies, resources, and news gathering.

REFERENCES

Belo Corp. (2002). 2002 annual report. Retrieved April 16, 2004, from http://www.belo.com

Belo Corp. (2003). 2003 annual report. Retrieved April 16, 2004, from http://www.belo.com

Belo Interactive Dallas. (n.d.). Brochure. Dallas, Texas.

Carlton, C. (2003, August 10). Belo interactive rolling out premium cowboys website. *The Dallas Morning News*, pp. C1, C5.

Finberg, H. (2004, November 15). Unwrapping news containers. Retrieved November 16, 2004, from http://www.poynter.org

Hass, T. (2000). Qualitative case study methods in newsroom research and reporting. In S. H. Iorio (Ed.), *Qualitative research in journalism: Taking it to the streets* (pp. 59–73). Mahwah, NJ: Lawrence Erlbaum Associates.

Murphy, J. (2002). Hard news for hard times. *MediaWeek, 12*(14), 21–26.

Securities and Exchange Commission. (2001). Form 10-K belo corp. Retrieved May 2, 2004, from http://www.sec.gov

Quick launches website. (2004, September 16). News release. Retrieved October 1, 2004, from http://www.belo.com

Zavoina, S., & Reichert, T. (2000). Media convergence/management change: The evolving workflow for visual journalists. *Journal of Media Economics, 13*(2), 143–151.

Conclusion

7

Social Capital: Implications for Convergence

These are interesting times as technological innovations enhance our ability to communicate through a myriad of channels. A casual stroll across any university campus will find students with heads tilted and cell phones seemingly permanently connected to their ears. A look around the gate area at any airport will show people working on laptops, watching CNN on the TV, reading the newspaper, playing with hand-held video games, using Blackberrys and cell phones, or, by chance, actually talking to the person sitting next to them. Indeed, we do communicate differently with an array of technology choices. However, it is not only the communication channels that have changed; a pertinent question is why we are selecting certain channels. The sociocultural implications for convergence perhaps lie in how we may or may not connect with each other because of the technological device we choose to channel our communication. I am by no means a technological determinist—someone who, according to Chandler's (1995) definition, suggests that technology drives social change. Quite the contrary, I view emerging technologies as tools that enhance and provide new channels of communication for innovators, producers, and manufacturers to bring to market, and individuals can choose whether to attend to those channels. The transformative relationship created by technology allows the individual to be proactive in selection of channels and content, and it forces traditional media gatekeepers to work harder at trying to determine what content or devices might interest the public.

Although a great deal of discussion on convergence may focus on journalism, salient to the convergence process is which newspaper, broadcast, and online entities are integrated to distribute content as well as other forms and tools of communication (Killebrew, 2002)? Whether it is by cell phone, the Internet, cable, satellite, PDAs, or a host of hand-held devices, people are exchanging information across platforms and in a variety of ways. A discussion follows in this chapter on some of the issues to consider when examining the impact of convergence beyond content providers to audience, society, and our culture. The discussion includes six areas: (a) sociocultural convergence, (b) journalism practices, (c) popular culture, (d) teaching convergence, (e) regulation, and (f) technological determinism.

SOCIOCULTURAL CONVERGENCE

The ambiguity that surrounds convergence raises discussions of its social implications. This is apparent in the uncertainty of how to define *convergence* as discussed in chapter 1. Once an organization or individuals agree on an approach to defining convergence, determining the process must follow. Convergence raises sociocultural concerns because as audiences continue to fragment media organizations pursue the splintered audiences with diverse offerings. The traditional media channels of print and broadcast have been integrated with the Internet to increase the opportunities to reach a diverse audience. The final delivery mode for content and products varies across organizations. It has become apparent that there is a pursuit to reach people with content when they want it and how they want it. Traditional print or broadcast outlets must face the question of whether they are in the content business or the newspaper, TV, or radio business. More are responding to the former and trying to deliver content across multiple platforms to meet a fragmented audience that is distracted and constantly changing because of the new array of choices.

Jenkins (2001) at the MIT Media Lab suggested that all media cannot be condensed and delivered conveniently in one box. He posited five types of convergence—technological, economic, social,

global, and cultural—as key to our understanding of how convergence works in our changing environment. For purposes of discussion here, we look closely at two areas that Jenkins described as
social/organic convergence and cultural convergence to examine
the impact of new technologies on society. Jenkins defines so-
cial/organic convergence as

> consumers' multitasking strategies for navigating the new informa-
> tion environment. Organic convergence is what occurs when a high
> schooler (sic) is watching baseball on a big-screen television, listen-
> ing to techno on the stereo, word-processing a paper and writing
> e-mail to his friends. It may occur inside or outside the box, but ulti-
> mately, it occurs with the user's cranium. (p. 93)

Thus, social convergence translates into the interactions that an
individual chooses to manage his or her media and information environment. Arguably, the concept of multitasking is viewed in many
ways, but often means conducting several tasks simultaneously,
such as using an exercise machine while accessing the Internet or
listening to music and watching TV (Kramer & Bernhardt, 1999;
Taylor, 1999). The individual has the option to watch TV, use the
Internet, and make a telephone call simultaneously. That person
makes a choice to either neglect one or incorporate all of the activities. The interest in accomplishing everything at once leads to the
multitasking perspective in use of new technologies.

According to Jenkins (2001), new technologies are increasing
our ability to accomplish multiple tasks at one time. However, he
does not suggest that we accomplish all of these tasks well. I agree
with this contention. The implications for social interaction could
be neglect in one area with too many activities at once or, for some,
an increased sense of accomplishment when communicating
through several channels. What might be occurring to a greater de-
gree is that socially we feel that we have accomplished more
through newer communication and telecommunication channels.
However, we do not know whether our use of these technologies is
effective in all settings. The social effects of communication
through mediated versus face-to-face channels has been the focus
of some research (Bordia, 1997; Hancock, & Dunham, 2001;

Kraut, Patterson, Lundmark, Kiesler, Mukopadhyay, & Scherlis, 1998; Tanis & Postmes, 2003; Walther, 1996). Obviously, face to face is richer than mediated communication, but expediency, forming community, and interactivity are reasons that some have found the Internet and other channels beneficial (Matei & Ball-Rokeach, 2003; Tanis & Postmes, 2003).

From a cultural perspective, there may be humanistic aspects of our lives that we are trading off due to the convenience of technology. Face-to-face communication may be negatively impacted if we develop social norms that eschew such contact in the name of expediency with technology. One does not supersede the other, but they perhaps coexist in an intimate relationship of need, purpose, and time. Newer networked technologies are pervasive and impact all aspects of our lives from work to home and play. The balancing act of how to integrate the areas could be a Herculean task, but individuals have gravitated to traditional media, converged media, and telecommunications devices according to their needs. The cultural implication of technology is how it is incorporated into our lives and for what reasons.

We turn to Jenkins' (2001) definition of *cultural convergence*, which is,

> the explosion of new forms of creativity at the intersections of various media technologies, industries and consumers. Media convergence fosters a new participatory folk culture by giving average people the tools to archive, annotate, appropriate and recirculate content. Shrewd companies tap this culture to foster consumer loyalty and generate low-cost content. Media convergence also encourages trans-media story-telling, the development of content across multiple channels. (p. 93)

Thus, the media industry and the public have a multitude of choices for sending and receiving different types of content. What might be of particular interest in this area of cultural convergence is the opportunity that has been created for the traditional consumer of media to become a producer. New technologies have transformed the relationship of the public to become more active in numerous ways. A computer, modem, creativity, and time are the ingredients for individuals to develop their own channels of communication. Developing a Web site is no longer a horrendous task requiring extensive knowledge of hyper text markup language (HTML), but an opportunity to land a place among millions of Web pages to share information. A Web site allows an array of people and their causes to become sources and distributors of information.

Whether it is online chats, Web sites, or Web blogs, numerous tools exist to connect one to one or one to many. Blogs are online journals in reverse chronological order that allow the producer to create an exchange of dialogue on any topic and post it on the Web. Blogs present a new context for understanding the role between journalists and the public, where the latter has the potential to become more involved, interactive, and a producer of information (Mattheson, 2004; Mintz, 2005). The new paradigm is the interactivity and two-way communication that is permissible with our new tools. Individuals are empowered to select a channel of communication that best suits their motivations and needs. Perhaps as Jenkins (2001) suggested, it will not be in one box or shop. We may continue to consider our cable, cell phones, newspapers, telephones, computers, and TV mediums as disparate channels. However, we may be attracted to their increased accessibility due to convergence processes that integrate these platforms.

I see this cultural change as part of what I call the new media information palette (MIP). The analogy would be the artist's palette of paints, in which a choice of colors is available to mix and mingle for the final masterpiece. The MIP allows the audience—*user, viewer, reader*, or *consumer* in the sea of interchangeable terms—to proactively select technology devices that meet their needs and motivations. From their MIP choices, the audience creates a kaleidoscope of media and communication technology customized to their individual needs. For example, instant messaging and photo cell phones with e-mail alerts may be more conducive to 18- to 24-year-olds for being connected and informed. Although baby boomers can enjoy the convenience of their cell phones, they continue to include TV and newspapers as part of their media information palette.

JOURNALISM PRACTICES

Cultural signposts are apparent as we watch the change in the media environment due to convergence facilitating the adaptation of certain processes within an organization. The argument throughout this book has been that convergence is both a concept and a process. The convergence process is not an end unto itself, but rather is continuous, adjusting, and adapting to the contours of an organization. Convergence is not static. The convergence process dictates changes for working journalists as well as managers and executives to adapt to their new environment. For example, a study on the change in workflow for visual journalists as a result of converged operations revealed efforts to integrate off- and online versions of media products for consistency in developing formats (Zavoina & Reichert, 2000). The study identified several issues such as lack of industry standards for publishing visuals on- and offline, heightened decision-making authority for smaller online staffs for visuals, more visuals in offline publications than online, and online visuals being cropped to meet the medium (Zavoina & Reichert, 2000). The two models the authors noted were the anomaly of an online publication working with the offline publication to coordinate visuals. However, the majority of arrangements occurred in which the online publication uses resources of the offline with little communication (Zavonia & Reichert, 2000). This study of visual communication is just one example of the on- and offline worlds and the changes that occurred as convergence processes started to increase for print, broadcast, and online platforms at media organizations.

As organizations integrate resources and content, the pursuit of the best application of this process becomes imperative. An example here is a study of the adoption of interactivity in three online newsrooms—*The New York Times, Houston Chronicle,* and *New Jersey Online*—that explored the convergence process at Web sites for these publications (Boczkowski, 2004). The focus was on the adoption of multimedia and interactivity for specific components of the online versions of the media organizations. The study specifically addressed the variations in organizational structures, organizational practices, and representations of users that contributed to the technology, adoption, and eventual effect on what was distributed in the content. In each instance, the media organization utilized specific components that treated interactivity to suit the content and audience for its online location. The needs and markets were different, so there is no specific catch-all formula or model that fits every organization at this time. Perhaps this is the way it should be to avoid homogeneity in content and approach. If each converged market is challenged to develop representations across platforms that meet the needs of that market, we avoid cookie cutter, one-size-fits-all convergence in a box.

POPULAR CULTURE

Convergence crosses into more than journalism practices in print, broadcast, and online. It is a part of popular culture that includes movies, CDs, video games, clothing, new devices, and much more. The Apple iPod allows the user to download music from preferred artists onto a portable device that enables the individual to listen whenever and wherever he or she wants. People are finding cross-promotion of products and services all around them. Integrating the use of various media devices can communicate numerous messages from a new pair of shoes with a music CD enclosed, to a new movie that includes video game characters (Yerton, 2003). Economic and technological forces are coming together to make everyone from media, telecommunications, and video game producers to music and those in the arts rethink combining forces. Thus, the media information palette (MIP) discussed earlier in this chapter is applicable to the audience that selects among these venues. The content media producers, electronic manufacturers, PC makers, and so on must determine the best practices that will help them reach individuals making their communication and media palette choices.

The potential for converging and cross-promoting across mediums was evidenced in the promotions for the 2004 Disney movie, "The Incredibles." This animated film included commercials, product tie-ins, and promotions with telecommunications and fast-food companies. The super-hero movie characters were featured in commercials on new broadband Internet connections for SBC Yahoo, used in the marketing of a $10 million sweepstakes, and promoted with McDonald's happy meals. The film's ability to impact audiences increased through this multimedia approach, and the movie's opening weekend brought in a noteworthy $70.7 million. This is indicative of what can happen with the convergence of mediums facilitated by technology. Brad Bird, the writer-director for the film, contended that, "Each medium has strengths and weaknesses" (cited in Westbrook, 2004). It is a matter of exploiting the best of technology through the appropriate platforms for an integrated product. The transformation in the relationship today is that the content producers cannot make the choice alone; the audience or consumer also has the potential to be a producer, therefore making media choices based on their needs, desires, and motivations. Mass media force-feeding choices is becoming less and less of a factor in the new millennium.

The effect of technology on popular culture through the integration of mediums is also evident in the growth of the video gaming industry. Traditional video arcades are part of the past as hand-held video games and cartridges for home game machines have increased the industry's potential. It is common now to see people not only playing games on the Internet, but a multitude of games on their cell phones as well. The top video games, such as *Grand Theft Auto* and *Tomb Raider*, are sold as cartridges for use in consoles for Sony, PlayStation 2, or X-box. But video games have an audience online, and producers are also taking advantage of women becoming a growing part of that group. AOL and Microsoft both provide online gaming and have taken note of the fact that women over age 35 are a growing part of their audience (Harrison, 2004). The content producers have altered their online gaming Web sites to take advantage of this audience.

Even traditional phone companies want in on the convergence game. Edward Whitacre, chairman and CEO of SBC Communications, drew industry and popular press interest in 2004 when he stated that the phone company should get in the TV business (cited in Latour, 2004). Whitacre contended that the industry and competition are changing the playing field for traditional phone providers, and he wanted SBC to offer phone, wireless, Internet, and video to customers. His goal is to "transform SBC into a state-of-the-art communications and TV giant that will have a dominant presence in consumers' living rooms" (cited in Latour, 2004, p. B1). Whitacre identified five reasons that people should receive TV from their phone company:

Reason 1: Phone companies have a trustworthy reputation.

Reason 2: Phone companies already offer TV via partnerships with satellite companies and can't keep up with demand.

Reason 3: Cable companies have a tradition of raising prices every year.

Reason 4: SBC would likely offer cable channels a la carte.

Reason 5: Consumers who buy all their services from SBC would get a big discount. (cited in Latour, 2004, p. B1)

Whitacre's corporate-speak today may translate into convergence that creates new communication frontiers tomorrow. A cautionary tale to remember is that when AT&T bought TCI Communications in 1999, the phone company wanted to get in the cable business offering broadband services. The convergence of phone and cable was not successful, and in 2002 Comcast's purchase of AT&T cable holdings was approved by the FCC. A cable company returned to manage a cable company. Lessons were learned, but technology, distribution, and processing have changed. The benefits of convergence are that it places the brand, product, and message on multiple platforms and transcends traditional processes of reaching the public. Whitacre and others may have communication and telecommunications crystal balls that foresee a change in the face of content and media products through the process of convergence.

TEACHING CONVERGENCE

If we are accessing and using media in new ways, then the people who teach and train those who collect and develop content will see changes as well. Journalism programs across the country are working to develop an online perspective or revamping curriculums to reflect a converged world. One example of this change in curriculum is apparent at Ball State University in Indiana, where the telecommunications program received a boost to convergence education and training through a $20 million grant from the Lilly Endowment (Horan, 2003). The grant was designated for upgrading telecommunications facilities and equipment and providing educational and research support. The environment for students includes five TV studios, high-definition camcorders, 14 video-editing bays, a video graphics lab, a multimedia classroom, and a computer lab with an electronic newsroom and teleconferencing capabilities. The program seeks to prepare graduates for the market with a competitive advantage and practical skills. Students produce material that is not only broadcast on campus, but also via cable into the local community.

Ball State's Center for Media Design (CMD) in the fall of 2004 released the first of a three-part study of convergence. The CMD received a 25% response rate in a national survey that translated into 372 newspaper editors responding to an examination of newspaper and TV convergence relationships. The results indicate that 30% of those newspapers are in some type of relationship promoting content with a TV outlet. The study found, however, that some newspapers are not taking advantage of all of the potential for collaborating with TV. Some findings from the study include:

- Separate corporations own newspaper and TV station partners in an overwhelming percentage of cases.
- Newspapers are willing to share story budgets and lineups with their broadcast partners, but they are mindful of a need to maintain a competitive edge by holding back stories that might be considered exclusives.
- About a quarter of partnerships plan special projects together at least four times a year. They frequently share the costs of those projects and coordinate release of the results. (Newsroom Partnership, 2004)

In contrast, the case studies in chapters 4 through 6 focused only on convergence operations in Chicago, Tampa, and Dallas, where broadcast and print outlets are owned by the same corporate parent company in each market. This has allowed for more sharing of resources, planning and promotion in different ways than the partnerships, and alliances in some of the markets for the Ball State study. This suggests that the FCC's removal in 2003 of the media cross-ownership rule for newspapers and TV stations in the same market, as well as other regulations, could have facilitated change in some markets. However, as noted earlier, the FCC action was repealed by a federal court in 2004, and the future of the cross-ownership rule is being closely watched. In numerous markets, newspapers and TV stations welcome the prospect of cross-ownership and the potential it might offer for convergence if outlets are owned by the same company, changing the competition paradigm. Where this will lead is unclear as industry and scholars watch for the next actions of the FCC on cross-ownership of media outlets in the same market.

College educators must also decide what it means to teach convergence. Decisions must be made on what a convergence curriculum should entail, what is to be included, and if moving forward on curriculum changes is the best approach (Birge, 2004). Criado and Kraeplin (2003) surveyed administrators of journalism programs, newspaper executives, and TV news managers to ascertain how convergence journalism was being handled. They found that convergence is viewed as important to the future of journalism, and that 9 out of 10 college administrators surveyed include or have started to include cross-platform training in their curriculum. Educators suggest that the demand for skills will increase as convergence becomes more of a norm in media operations. Of educators, 31% "believe that being trained in more than one medium" will be important for students applying for jobs (Criado & Kraeplin, 2003, p. 9). The study also found that 95% of newspapers and 83% of TV stations in the study had created convergence partnerships. The findings touch on the growing significance of converged media operations and preparing future journalists with skills to work in such environments.

It is too early to determine how university and college curriculums and training for convergence will work best. There is a growing movement to transition journalism programs to include some aspect of convergence in the curriculum. Teaching multimedia journalism is a natural outgrowth of watching changes in the industry. After a year of study, the faculty at Northwest Missouri University decided there was a need for the curriculum to offer some multimedia components as they watched media convergence ascending in the industry (cited in Sudhoff & Donnelly, 2003). The eight faculty members teach four sequences: broadcasting, print journalism, advertising, and digital media design. One faculty member cautioned, "Curriculum should be sensitive to important theoretical and conceptual matters, and not just the latest technical trend" (p. 63). Thus, the faculty developed a consensus for direction of the curriculum after numerous meetings, input from industry and an advisory board, and examining programs at other schools. The programs at the University of Kansas, Indiana University, and the University of Southern California–Annenberg are among many that have moved in the direction of curriculum changes to incorporate a convergence perspective in training students.

In *Online Journalism Review*, Castañeda (2003) addressed some concerns that come with changing school curriculums. Castañeda noted that these areas must be considered: defining convergence for faculty and students, emphasizing shared journalistic values, avoiding the creation of super reporters, learning new skills, seeking geeks, and slowing down to speed up. Castañeda advocated researching, preparing, and continuing to develop a convergence curriculum for the best fit. This process is not based on assumption, but trying to understand what will work for a curriculum to help students grasp the multimedia environment. Journalism schools do not want to risk their reputations and hobble out some unsatisfactory program, but to be recognized as "the" school that would offer students the best in journalism training (Birge, 2004). Without question, educators and professionals emphasize the basic fundamentals of good writing, news judgment, and values as the cornerstone to any program.

Of course there have been critics of the "backpack journalist" who would walk around with a reporter's notepad, camera, and video recorder—the jack of all trades. Media managers are not in search of that type of journalists, but rather someone who is trained in his or her craft and aware and capable of being trained to work in a multimedia environment. The multimedia dimension includes understanding different ways of storytelling across platforms once the foundations of journalism are in place. The future for students studying convergence will not only be the jobs available, but the regulatory environment that may support or restrict convergence efforts across the country.

REGULATION

FCC Chairman Michael Powell (2003) has been both praised and scorned for his role as head of the regulatory agency for broadcast and telecommunications media. Powell is firmly entrenched in FCC regulations adapting to the market for broadcasters and technological changes that have occurred over the years. Broadcast media previously included TV and radio, but now includes cable, telephones, wireless, and satellite. The 1996 Telecommunications Act relaxed many of the regulatory rules for broadcast and telecommunications. The goal was that competition would increase and cross-ownership would occur. Instead, a concentrated media environment flourished and more media outlets are owned by fewer corporate entities. Powell suggested this is not necessarily bad and the market will determine which media outlets will prevail. After the 1996 Telecom Act, Congress required the FCC to review its rules biennially. The FCC did and in 2003, led by Powell, voted to end the cross-ownership rule that allowed newspaper and TV stations to be owned by the same company in one market, increased the broadcast ownership cap from 35% to 45% of the United States, and instituted other deregulations for broadcasters and radio.

Powell (2003) contended that change is necessary because the current media environment is not the same as it was for traditional media 20 or even 10 years ago. Radio, broadcast, and cable were the focus until satellite, the Internet, and newer technologies increased media choices. Powell suggested that the public interest is his focus when pressing for changes to FCC regulations he deems necessary to the future. He cited five reasons that change in the industry must occur. According to Powell (2003):

> First, it is important for us to rebuild our media regulatory regime in order to get a coherent and internally consistent set of rules that more correctly reflect the media landscape and the rich and varied ways consumers and citizens get their information.... Second, change may be imperative if we want to preserve free over the air television.... Third, while many view big as always antithetical to the public interest, scale and efficiency are becoming more vital to delivering quality news and public affairs.... Fourth, digital migration. Media is itself changing as a new digital world unfolds.... Fifth, diversity itself. More capacity may allow producers to respond to increased customer fragmentation and competition for viewers and listeners. (pp. 6–7)

Although Powell's arguments have merit, such prolific critics as Robert McChesney, Ben Bagdikian, and Mark Crispin Miller contend that the FCC stepping aside and allowing more deregulation to occur in the broadcast industry would be harmful to democracy and a mix of voices in the public sphere. This is a concern in that, if media elite theory holds true, the ownership of most of the media by a powerful few could limit the diversity of voices in the public sphere. There are anecdotal examples of corporate leaders influencing content of media outlets owned by the parent company, but no overwhelming evidence of industry efforts to limit choice in content has been found. Here is where Powell stated that the market would take hold and competition would fill in the void. Convergence discussions are critical because they would center on large media companies that have concentrated ownership in print, broadcast, and online and, thus, would have a larger forum for their distribution process. If big media has more outlets, how many voices will the public hear?

Some of this might be unsettling to opponents of concentrated ownership of media outlets, but proponents contend that competition will ensure that multiple voices are heard. For example, in a market such as New York, one organization should not be able to limit coverage. The major TV networks are all headquartered in New York, and if one combination of newspaper, broadcast, and online ownership chooses to avoid or limit coverage on a topic, other media outlets in New York would quickly step in and fill the void. This may be true in large markets with a number of media organizations, but what happens in Peoria, Illinois, or Paducah, Kentucky? These are small, local markets that do not have an array of media choices.

The industry is watching to see what will happen with the cross-ownership rule once the FCC addresses the federal court's concerns and is able to move forward. In chapter 1, we discussed The American Press Institute's Convergence Tracker, which is a self-reported collection of convergence partnerships and alliances around the country. Because the FCC ban on cross-ownership remains in place, more alliances and partnerships exist than actual ownership by one parent company of different media in the same market. The Ball State University newspaper and TV partnership study also notes this phenomenon. However, concerns are being raised if the rule change by the FCC would prompt more ownership changes instead of a continuation of current arrangements. The concern over limited voices with decreased ownership immediately follows this discussion. To date this has not been the case, but what will occur is uncertain. The regulatory process is viewed as a catch basin to ensure that no media company becomes the all-encompassing channel in a given market. No one knows what the media ownership landscape will look like with more deregulation. What is for certain is that the industry will continue to adjust and adapt to a changing technology environment and audience of users, viewers, readers, or consumers of different types of media.

TECHNOLOGICAL DETERMINISM

Another effect of technology on society suggested earlier in this chapter has been the issue of technological determinism. Chandler (1995) stated:

> The technological determinist view is a technology-led theory of social change: technology is seen as the "prime mover" in history. According to technological determinists, particular technical developments, communication technologies or media, or most broadly, technology in

general are the sole or prime antecedent cause of change in society, and technology is seen as the fundamental condition underlying the pattern of social organization. Technological determinists interpret technology in general and communications technologies in particular as the basis of society in the past, present and even the future. They say that technologies such as writing or print or television or the computer "changed society." In its most extreme form, the entire form of society is seen as being determined by technology: new technologies transform society at every level, including institutions, social interaction and individuals. At the least, a wide range of social and cultural phenomena are seen as shaped by technology. "Human factors" and social arrangements are seen as secondary. (p. 2)

Karl Marx, Alvin Toffler, and Nicholas Negroponte are sometimes associated with discussions of technology as a catalyst driving society (Gunkel, 2003). However, despite the compelling notion of technological determinism, I do not support this view of emerging technologies. The history of our society has been one of innovation and development. The digital technology proliferating today is indicative of the time and society's reaction. Just because it is built does not mean everyone will come. There are plasma TVs and razor-thin, hand-held electronic devices. Yet for every sale that is made, there are individuals who cling to the traditional telephone and analog TV, or prefer their daytimer to an electronic calendar. The price of personal computers has decreased, and people are attracted to the novelty of phones with Web capabilities and PDAs with attachable key pads. The clear picture and high resolution of high-definition TV (HDTV) have been under discussion, and even the FCC has required that broadcasters convert all of their analog broadcasts to digital by 2006. This was part of the digital spectrum giveaway to broadcasters in 1996, instead of the potential $70 billion in revenue that could have been generated for charging for the spectrum. Broadcasters are still behind in converting to digital, and the public is slow to turn to $1,500 TV sets to watch HDTV. Yet there is a coexistence of analog and digital devices to date based on interest, need, and price. The innovators, manufacturers, and distributors may push for research and development to continue the pursuit of the next great technology device. Yet the individual—the consumer of technology—is primary in the marketplace in determining which items will have longevity. The audience has their media information palette to choose from and are empowered by the knowledge that what is adopted and stays in the market reflects more of their use and need, rather than the producers' marketing, advertising, and promotion strategies.

Two types of technological determinism have been identified: "hard determinism makes technology the sufficient or necessary condition for social change, while soft determinism understands technology to be a key factor that may facilitate change" (Gunkel, 2003, p. 510). Negroponte (1995) clearly identified the bits and atoms of digital technology that have accelerated the information process. Toffler (1980) noted what the waves of an agricultural, industrial, and information society driven by new technologies have brought. However, rather than hard determinism, I suggest that the more suitable approach for today's environment would be soft determinism, where technology facilitates a change. The rapid innovations and the unlimited possibilities may have increased the amount and types of media and communication devices coming our way; however, we have not completely abandoned established and traditional tools. History dictates that media and communication technology have coexisted (e.g., telephones and cell phones, newspapers and radio, cable and TV), and I predict they will do so in the future. The discussion in chapter 3 on innovations in organizations addresses this in terms of how organizations adapt to change. Although technology is constantly changing, adopting new tools and ideas is not a fast-paced process within an organization. Individuals are similar in their attraction to trinkets and the novelty of certain new technologies, but without widespread adoption one person's ability to digitize content on their cell phone disconnects if there are not enough people adopting the same device. Failed technologies discussed in chapter 3 had limited shelf lives for countless reasons.

The media industry has been impacted by technology in terms of the process of gathering and disseminating information (Boczkowski, 2004). Gutenberg's 15th-century discovery of movable type led to the revolution of mass production. Each technological advancement along the way provided media a new opportunity to increase its reach. When typewriters began to fade out of news-rooms by the 1980s, it was not always a rapid process. The adoption of video display terminals (VDTs) and the eventual move to computers with pagination for design and layout was not broadly accepted in the early years. In the media industry, however, different media outlets seek to provide the type of content that the audience needs and wants. There is no exact formula for determining that need, therefore, as in the case of the convergence process; there is a great deal of trial and error. What may be offered offline in print or broadcast might find another forum in an online presentation. People have changed how and what media they use, and content providers of all types seek to adapt.

As discussed earlier in this chapter, the 2004 movie *The Incredibles* utilized technological advances of computers to develop animated characters. The producers also utilized multiple platforms to promote a story for the movie screen that originated in a print comic book. In contrast, although the computer appeared to be a natural medium for distribution of music, the leading music companies did not initially take advantage of the medium. Instead the companies created a legal battle to shut down Napster and other file-sharing organizations on the Internet. The Recording Industry of America filed numerous lawsuits against those caught illegally downloading. Once the potential to download music accelerated, however, music companies identified the potential revenue lost and wanted to reap the economic benefit of distributing music online if their audiences sought the distribution channel. Since Apple started a fee for downloading of music coupled with its iPod music device, a new converged arrangement developed for accessing and enjoying music. These are examples of how convergence has created new processes and products by media, computer, and electronic manufacturers.

The cultural implications of convergence center more on the possible decrease—rather than increase—of face-to-face communication among individuals. The Internet has been cited for its potential to facilitate or weaken social bonds (Matei & Ball-Rokeach, 2003). Imagine this potential when the Internet is converged with other mediums. At present, individuals are taken with the myriad media and communication choices and choose accordingly. A Time Warner cable subscriber may select that medium to receive broadcasts, but may not choose *Time* magazine or any other member of parent company Time Warner for media use. Yet industry executives would like to provide phone, cable, wireless, Internet, broadcast, and print information and entertainment needs under one umbrella. This has not been the case thus far. An individual chooses one company for her cell phone and service and another for broadcast, selects something different for a newspaper or magazine, and buys music from the artist of preference regardless of the music company.

We do not know at this time how all of the technological innovations will shake out in the media and communication arena. Even discussions of the digital divide of haves and have-nots' access to the technology available are starting to change (Gunkel, 2003). The competitive marketplace has resulted in a decrease in the cost of computers and Internet provider services. Public libraries, schools and other institutions are providing access to computers and Internet resources. Even some municipalities are pushing to provide wireless fidelity (Wi-Fi) service to communities to increase the possibility for access to the Internet by even more people.

SUMMARY

The sociocultural implications of convergence lie more in how the different media technologies are used in society. This is a process I contend will be driven by individuals more than media or computer and electronic manufacturers. The providers offer the choice of content and products, but individuals determine what remains in the market. Media organizations have an economic investment in trying to provide content any time, any place, and through any platform for their audiences. The tenets of good journalism are espoused, and research to date has not shown blatant violations of such practices. The possibilities of emerging technologies raise more interest if the channels of communication supersede the audience and intent.

It may be unclear at this moment where all of these changes will lead us in the future. However, what is clear now is that media organizations and the public are actively pursuing use of new technology devices for a variety of reasons. Which components will become more useful and remain with us along the lines of TV instead of the telegraph is not certain. We may outgrow some of our communication devices or retire them for lack of efficiency or interest. The strength of the media information palette I posit is that the individual user is in control and makes the final decision on which technologies are included in their package. The telegraph was a precursor to the communication devices that followed and moved to its place in the technology timeline. However, new technologies are developed so rapidly that we do not adjust to a cell phone before the photo phone appears and then the Blackberry. The principle of relative constancy regarding spending on technology suggests we will spend only a certain percentage of money on media, and competing new technologies must work within that pool of money. Of course there will always be early adopters of technology who purchase the first plasma TV, new Blackberry, or DVD player. The majority of users, however, will make choices on what dollars are available to spend on technology and shift priorities for devices based on the available funds. Yet the sociocultural implications of convergence are not necessarily negative. We are communicating and interacting in different ways. For some, e-mail, blogs, and chats may provide an immediacy and connectivity that suits certain environments. For others, cross-promotion of content and products across print, broadcast, and online may be more fulfilling than hit or miss in one medium. The technological tools are intriguing and useful, but which tools will stay or go will be determined by individuals in society and the utility and reliability of certain technological innovations in communication and media over those that are less useful. The rapid and simultaneous development of new technologies has changed the paradigm. We may be on the cycle of using new technologies sooner, but they, in turn, may die off if their utility is not sustained.

REFERENCES

Birge, E. (2004). Teaching convergence—but what is it? Educators struggle with ambiguous definitions from the profession. *Feedback, 45*(6), 36–43.

Boczkowski, P. J. (2004). The process of adopting multimedia and interactivity in three online newsrooms. *Journal of Communication, 54,* 197–213.

Bordia, P. (1997). Face-to-face versus computer-mediated communication: A synthesis of the experimental literature. *Journal of Business Communication, 34,* 99–120.

Castañeda, L. (2003, March 6). Teaching convergence. *Online Journalism Review.* Retrieved March 31, 2003, from http://www.ojr.org

Chandler, D. (1995). Technological or media determinism. Retrieved October 30, 2004, from http://www.aber.ac.uk/media/Documents/tecdet/tecdet.html

Criado, C. A., & Kraeplin C. (2003). *The state of convergence journalism: United States media and university study.* Unpublished manuscript, Southern Methodist University.

Gunkel, D. J. (2003). Second thoughts. Toward a critique of the digital divide. *New Media & Society, 5*(4) 499–522.

Hancock, J. T., & Dunham, P. J. (2001). Impression formation in computer mediated communication revisited: An analysis of the breadth and intensity of impressions. *Communication Research, 28,* 325–347.

Harrison, C. (2004, March 10). Games women play: The over 35 set makes up two-thirds of participants at web sites. *The Dallas Morning News* [Electronic Version]. Retrieved March 11, 2004, from http://www.dallasnews.com

Horan, L. (2003). Considering convergence: Ball State moves toward merged media environment. *Government Video,* pp. 34–37.

Jenkins, H. (2001). Convergence? I diverge. *Technology Review, 104*(5), 93.

Killebrew, K. C. (2002). Culture, creativity and convergence: Managing journalists in a changing information workplace. *The International Journal on Media Management, 5*(1), 39–46.

Kramer, R., & Bernhardt, S. A. (1999). Moving instruction to the web: Writing as multitasking. *Technical Communication Quarterly, 8*(3), 319–336.

Kraut, R., Patterson, M., Lundmark, V., Kiesler, S., Mukopadhyay, T., & Scherlis, W. (1998). Internet paradox: A social technology that reduces social involvement and psychological well-being? *American Psychologist, 53*(9), 1017–1031.

Latour, A. (2004, November 23). Meet the new tv guy: SBC's whitacre revs up for video as cable, internet, eat into his phone business. *The Wall Street Journal,* pp. B1, B5).

Matei, S., & Ball-Rokeach, S. (2003). The internet in the communication infrastructure of urban residential communities: Macro- or meso-linkage? *Journal of Communication, 53*(4), 642–657.

Mattheson, D. (2004). Weblogs and the epistemology of the news: Some trends in online journalism. *New Media & Society, 6*(4), 443–468.

Mintz, J. (2005, January 21). When bloggers make news: As their clout increases, web diarists are asking: Just what are the rules? *The Wall Street Journal,* pp. B4, B1.

Negroponte, N. (1995). *Being digital.* New York: Vintage.

Newsroom partnership survey executive summary. (2004). Center for Media Design. Ball State University. Retrieved November 15, 2004, from http://www.bsu.edu

Powell, M. K. (2003). Remarks of Michael K. Powell Federal Communications Commission at the Media Institute, March 27, 2003. Retrieved April 1, 2003, from http://www.fcc.gov

Sudhoff, D., & Donnelly, J. (2003). Upgrading course offerings: Changing a curriculum can be a difficult task. *Quill, 91*(5), 62–63.

Tanis, M., & Postmes, T. (2003). Social cues and impression formation in cmc. *Journal of Communication, 53*(4), 676–693.

Taylor, C. P. (1999). Now, that's multi-tasking. *MediaWeek, 9*(11), 4.

Toffler, A. (1980). *The third wave.* New York: Bantam.

Walther, J. B. (1996). Computer-mediated communication: Impersonal, interpersonal, and hyperpersonal interaction. *Communication Research, 23*(1), 3–43.

Westbrook, B. (2004, November 7). Bird flies high with incredibles: But hand-drawn animation is not dead yet, insists writer-director. *Houston Chronicle* [Electronic Version]. Retrieved November 8, 2004, from http://www.chron.com/cs/CDA/ssistory.mpl/features/2889134

Yerton, S. (2003, October 26). Media convergence a prism for pop culture: The distinctions between media, and the lines between commerce and art, are fading into oblivion as the blending picks up pace. *The Oregonian* [Electronic Version]. Retrieved October 29, 2003, from http://www.oregonlive.com/printer/printer.ssf?/base/business/1066997056122540.xml

Zavoina, S., & Reichert, T. (2000). Media convergence: Management change: The evolving workflow for visual journalists. *Journal of Media Economics, 13*(2), 143–151.

8

The Future of Convergence

Where do we go from here? "Broadband is bringing us all together. You can combine all three elements. News is a 24-7 operation, and if you don't have the journalistic muscles in all three (fields), you can't succeed in broadband," according to Arthur O. Sulzberger Jr., chairman and publisher of New York Times Company (cited in Damewood, 2004, par. 7). Such a provocative statement from the head of an old-guard, traditional newspaper raises interest for its implication to the greater media industry. The stoic *New York Times* has increased its media holdings as well as its efforts for distribution of content across print, broadcast, and online. Sulzberger's comments may be only one view of the future for media convergence, but it is one that I support. Technological innovations over the past years have intertwined the use of new technology devices—hardware or software—with the industry's future.

Sulzberger's comments also serve as an example of a changing environment that has caused traditional media executives, particularly those in print, to step back and access where the industry is going. Readership of newspapers is down, TV networks are challenged by cable and satellite, and radio has Internet and satellite radio moving into its territory. Convergence is not a panacea for all the needs of media, but a choice among strategies for building for the next century.

Newspapers are pursuing numerous strategies from new products, zoned editions, product innovations, marketing programs, and convergence to reach their audiences. The same is true with broadcasters experimenting with new programs, (e.g., reality TV shows or coupling efforts with other media and online outlets). The

183

Internet and other new media devices are impacting the habits of TV audiences. Technological innovations are contributing to an increase in the ability to use different technologies to reach an increasingly fragmented media audience. The urge to converge may derive out of necessity and not just novelty of the times. Media uses and patterns have changed significantly, and owners do not want to sit by waiting for the next big thing to come. We know that media users multitask, as research indicates in our discussion of multi-uses of the Web. Such behavior leads content providers to the conclusion that they cannot be static. A continued drive toward innovation and adoption of different types of content and products to reach audiences is a necessity.

A preeminent storyteller, Don Hewitt, founding producer for CBS' *60 Minutes*, once wrote that the formula for his success in broadcasting was simple: "Tell me a story" (Hewitt, 2001). That is exactly what I tried to do in this book—to tell a story about convergence as a concept and a process at this point in time through the prism of three convergence pioneers in the media industry. Tribune, Media General, and Belo are not alone in the convergence journey for media organizations. They were selected to illustrate how, in the Chicago, Tampa, and Dallas markets, where there is cross-ownership of media properties, convergence as a concept and process has been given an opportunity to set a course for its future in journalism and the media industry. In this chapter, we discuss the future of convergence—albeit undetermined—and the signs and directions for the process.

My research dictates that convergence will continue to be a part of the future for the media industry. How it will manifest itself will keep analysts, industry executives, scholars, and critics watching and waiting. Empirical research will help to ascertain what aspects of convergence are gaining ground and which are falling by the wayside. Critics will keep the industry and academics on their toes, raising questions about the impact of concentrated ownership and convergence of diverse voices in the public sphere.

The future may be uncertain, but one thing is certain—emerging digital technologies will play a prominent role in future media and communication distribution. Nowhere in our history have we stepped back when technological innovations have propelled us forward—from the discovery of the wheel to Gutenberg's printing press, from video display terminals (VDTs) to computers and PCs, and from DVDs to the Internet and satellite. The media industry has been continuously impacted by technological changes, whether it embraced the change or delayed the inevitable, as some journalists attempted when they tried to hold on to their typewriters and grease pencils instead of moving to VDTs and PCs.

Convergence entails some hits and misses as discussed in the case studies on the convergence pioneers. However, there are some elements which suggest that the concept and process of convergence is here to stay. First, there are economies of scale that organizations feel compelled to take advantage of to improve operations. The sharing of resources, whether people or equipment, has proved beneficial. There are reductions in back office services in such areas as advertising and human resources by eliminating duplication and scaling down processes. Second, collaboration on the types of content and products distributed to the audience is enhanced through input from many voices instead of a few. However, there are some from both print and broadcast who find that convergence presents organizational culture and other practical challenges to be addressed. Finally, technology has advanced and improved the capabilities for media organizations to move content and resources between and among platforms. For example, content management tools such as BudgetBank in Tampa or Oxygen at Tribune Company in Chicago allow different business units to speak electronically. In other words, they can view each other's material that was previously stored on different software.

Technological barriers of incompatible systems had to be conquered to enable converging business units to communicate. In these examples, a parent company owns the converging partners, so access is feasible. However, in the larger convergence scenario of partnerships and alliances among media outlets, the participants are not owned by the same parent company and are not able to readily share information. Satellites and electronic feeds and servers in broadcast newsrooms have increased the capacity to upload and download the same material. No longer does someone have to wait for tape to be dubbed and physically transported. The use of shared servers, such as Tribune's Tribnet, allows broadcasters in convergence arrangements to take advantage of the shared-use process. The advent of digital video recorders (DVRs) allows broadcasters to capture material 24 hours a day for use at another time.

The verdict is still out, but recent findings suggest that journalists and others are warming to certain aspects of a converged environment (Boczkowski, 2004). Newsroom environments are changing as more organizations take advantage of the opportunities that sharing resources and content provide. Scholars are studying the implications of convergence to quantify and assess what may or may not work in the integrating of mediums for distributing content and products. There are some issues that will serve as signposts of what may be a part of the future of convergence. The seven issues discussed next are what I contend will be barometers in ascertaining how convergence will settle into the 21st century for the media industry and the public.

CONVERGENCE PIONEERS

Whether it is in Chicago, Tampa, or Dallas, the convergence process is moving forward. The parent companies of the print, broadcast, and Internet media outlets in these markets are in the position to act on their convergence impulses. This translates into efforts to integrate content and products that can occur with an expediency unlike that for other media organizations. Earlier in this book, we stated that Tribune, Media General, and Belo were selected as convergence pioneers case studies because they were grandfathered into the FCC's 1975 newspaper/broadcast cross-ownership rules. The companies already owned the cross-media properties before the ban went into effect and the newspapers and TV stations in those markets were allowed to continue operation and take advantage of any connections they chose to make. There are about 40 organizations grandfathered under the newspaper/broadcast cross-ownership rule (FCC Initiates, 2001). By the 1990s, when Internet use was gaining momentum, media outlets wanted to make their presence known online. Therefore, accompanying Web sites were created for newspapers, radio, and TV stations. The content of those sites evolved over the years to make way for shovelware, providing a duplicate of what appeared in the brick-and-mortar versions of the company.

Convergence as a process is more prolific in the daily operations and long-term strategies of the three case study organizations discussed in this book. Through internal and external actions, these organizations have identified that convergence is the way they do business and continue to evolve the types of content used for convergence. The concept and process of convergence may not sway everyone, but the organizations utilizing the process seek to capitalize on a changing, fragmented media market that seeks different things at different times. The objective is to allow the public access to whatever it might be looking for on whatever platform it can be delivered.

The future entails keeping an eye on the convergence pioneers and the directions they will take over the next several years. This book provides a snapshot, but the entire picture is not fully developed. What may work in Chicago might be viewed in a completely different way in another market. For example, Detroit has two newspapers in a joint operating agreement (JOA), *The Detroit News* and *The Detroit Free Press*, which have online representations of their newspapers. In the online environment streaming video, FLASH presentations and interactivity are incorporated for the audience experience. If a partnership or alliance were created with one of the local broadcast stations, would that extend the brand for either newspaper? Would people feel that news coverage was more inclusive if the print and broadcast outlets converged? Would broadcast outlets be attracted to partnerships with print for presentation of content across multiple platforms in the Detroit market? Each party would have to find value in a potential convergence arrangement. The audience would be the ultimate determinant if such arrangements are warranted and can be sustained.

The FCC media cross-ownership rule may be in limbo at this time, but what we should be watching in the industry is which media organizations create new convergence movements. If aggressive movements start to occur for partnerships and alliances in Detroit and other markets, then industry leaders are pushing the integration efforts forward regardless of the uncertainties about media ownership regulations. I expect convergence efforts to continue because of the changing nature of media markets and the fragmenting of audiences. Different people use different media at different times. Why? Because they can. No one is bound by network news, newspaper printing cycles, or artificial timelines. We watched the VCR lead to time shifting by allowing people to record and delay when they tuned into their news or programs of interests. The 24-hour, 7-day-a-week news cycle that has been created by the Internet, cable, and satellite does not appear to be slowing down. The more choices people have, the more they are willing to explore the possibilities. We do not know which formulas or combinations will work, but we do know that each media outlet, whatever the market, has a vested interested in trying to appease a diverse public in interest and technology use. It is not a matter of gadgets and gimmicks, but genuinely seeking a business model for convergence that is customized to the market. Currently, large cities have the advantage of choice in ways that smaller markets do not. Media in smaller markets do not have all the economic and people resources, but alliances and partnerships could reconfigure their positions in the equation. William Singleton, CEO of MediaNews Group, informed members of the National Newspaper Association at their 2004 convention that smaller and medium-sized papers may be better suited for convergence because they are easier and cheaper to buy in small markets (cited in Small Papers, 2004). There is strength in numbers, and smaller media markets will find outlets working to change the playing field to have a role in what convergence may or may not be in the future.

MULTIMEDIA STORIES

As discussed in chapter 1, the Convergence Tracker created by the American Press Institute provides a compilation of convergence partnerships and alliances nationwide. The Tracker list is not the definitive list on convergence, but illustrates the expansion of convergence as a process. Regardless of the market, media outlets that are attempting partnerships and alliances are getting their organizations in on some level of what may be the harbinger of the future. This is particularly important for newspapers that want to connect in different ways with their core audience and potential news audiences that might not have grown up on newspapers. Over the past decades, emerging technologies have groomed some people to move past newspapers because TV and Internet resources provide an immediate connection to news, information, and entertainment. It is not a value judgment if this is the right course for people to pursue. Rather, it is the accessibility and ease of use to which more people feel connected. For example, the 300th anniversary of the first successful newspaper—*The Boston News-Letter*—occurred in 2004 (Lenger, 2004). There was not much fanfare on the part of the casual observer, but journalists and scholars are aware of the significance and potential changes for newspapers in the future. The future of newspapers includes remembering barriers from the past (e.g., technology, labor, competition, start-up costs) and fending off challenges for the future (e.g., technology, labor, competition, obsoleteness). Lenger (2004) suggested that newspapers need to stay free of government control, try to minimize news monopolies, provide robust local news and less "infotainment" and sensationalism in news coverage, and increase their ability to embrace new technologies. The future of newspapers may depend on validating their relevance to audiences and making local connections to complementary media channels.

If the media does not tell its story of convergence and use of multimedia, it cannot expect the public to understand the significance of what is occurring in the industry. Gannett's corporate Web site, The Gannett News Department, http://newsdepartment.gannett.com, provides a portal for the latest on newspapers and new media. The site's multimedia link leads to examples of what the company considers good efforts in use of multimedia. These are not definitive examples, but were chosen to illustrate multimedia's ability to add another dimension for the audience and its added value over time. People want to feel there is some added value to connecting across platforms and following cross-promotion efforts.

In one example linked on the Gannett Web site, *The Springfield (Missouri) News-Leader* used FLASH graphics to draw the audience into a multimedia story on the city's $32 million ballpark, which is part of the city's downtown revitalization. The use of multimedia created storytelling that is accessible on- and offline, and the FLASH presentation of the ballpark provides photos and graphics for a close look at what the new stadium offers. Further, the multimedia package highlighted that this was more than a news story, but also a lifestyle and cultural issue for the changing community. In previous presentations, there would have been photos and graphics in the newspaper or video on TV. The multimedia presentations online allow for continuous access to different aspects of the story.

Another multimedia example from Gannett is the coverage by *The News Journal* in Wilmington, Delaware, of Hurricane Jeanne and a tornado that struck the area in September 2004. A visit to the Web site allows the audience to access the Web story, video, photos, and graphics that present the nuances of the weather's impact on the community. The audience may not use all aspects of the multimedia presentation, but they are provided an opportunity to understand the weather's impact from a range of angles. The electronic storytelling places convergence in a different context because it can be archived and recalled more readily by the audience. The audience is also able to select various elements of the multimedia package instead of an all-or-nothing approach.

The J-Lab—Institute for Interactive Journalism—at the University of Maryland, Philip Merrill School of Journalism was created to identify and support innovative journalism using technology. The J-Lab encourages use of technology and journalism to increase awareness of public affairs and to engage the public. The organization distributes the yearly Batten Award for Innovations in Journalism online. The awards, named for James Batten, former Knight-Ridder CEO, recognize organizations that use technology in innovative ways to get the public involved. The Web site provides numerous examples of award winners and others who have increased the discourse on public policy with Web sites that use multimedia and are highly interactive for the public. Whether it is a PBS station, commercial broadcaster, or newspaper, J-Lab points to work that is embracing new technology in ways that improve journalism, involve the public, and use technology.

The multimedia storytelling is where I contend that many media organizations in various markets will get their feet wet with convergence if they are not a fully converged operation. Whether media outlets are owned by a corporate parent or are in partnerships and alliances, they can utilize multimedia storytelling. The transformation into a completely converged operation may not be the object of all media organizations. This type of storytelling, particularly with breaking news and enterprising stories, presents the opportunity to experiment with different presentations of stories. It requires the openness and imagination of reporters, editors, photographers, and artists to push the presentation of news and information beyond traditional boundaries. The ability to expand those boundaries will include whatever lies on the horizon for regulation of media outlets that seek more integration of people, resources, and physical properties across print, broadcast, and online.

THE FCC MEDIA CROSS-OWNERSHIP RULE

When the FCC voted on June 2, 2003, to lift the ban on the newspaper/broadcast cross-ownership rule, there was immediate appreciation for the vote by owners and executives in the media industry. It was a long anticipated and lobbied process that media wanted to happen. Since 1975, when the ban was enacted, newspapers and broadcasters that were not grandfathered into the rule have waited for the change. The FCC lifting of the ban was brief because the Commission was immediately challenged by a lawsuit from several disparate watchdog groups and advocates. It was not until the summer of 2004 that the FCC learned the federal court in Philadelphia would reject the ban and send them back to reassess where to go next.

First, let us briefly examine what the FCC's 2003 vote would have allowed once the cross-ownership ban was lifted. A summary of the decisions by the FCC in 2003 include:

- In markets with nine or more TV stations, eliminated the broadcast-newspaper and the radio-TV cross-ownership rules. In markets with four to eight stations, combinations are limited. In markets with three or fewer TV stations, no cross-ownership is permitted among TV, radio, and newspapers.
- Continued the current limits on radio station ownership in markets.
- Increased the national TV ownership from a 35% limit to a 45% limit for reaching U.S. households.
- Retained the ban on mergers among any of the top four national broadcast networks.
- Set the local TV multiple ownership rule at 2 stations (duopoloy) with markets that have 5 or more stations and at 3 stations (triopoloy) in markets with 18 or more stations.

Although these rule changes were struck down in federal court, future FCC actions on these changes are important to watch as they relate to the expansion of convergence processes. Arguments have been made on both sides that, without cross-ownership, there will be a rush to buy up newspapers and broadcast stations for joint ownership in the same market. We will not know the strength or weakness of this argument until such a day occurs. An analysis by investment house Bear Stearns (2003) provided some insight into the potential impact on the media industry if the cross-ownership ban is eventually removed. The New York investors identified several potential scenarios for changes in the industry if cross-ownership of newspaper and broadcast outlets is permitted. First, removal of the FCC rule would prohibit cross-ownership in 31 of the 210 designated market areas (DMAs). These are markets with three or fewer TV stations such as Glendive, Montana; Bend, Oregon; or Utica, New York. However, this provides the potential for cross-ownership of print and broadcast in 107 markets with four to eight TV stations. In markets of nine stations or more—about 72 markets—cross-ownership would still be prohibited. The Bear Stearns report suggests that newspapers benefit from the removal of the cross-ownership ban because it would provide opportunities to diversify in local markets. Readership is down, as well as advertising revenue changes, so newspapers would welcome expansion opportunities. The report suggests that Gannett and Tribune would probably be the media companies to pursue acquisitions if the FCC cross-ownership ban were to materialize (Bear Stearns, 2003).

It is not a matter of if, but when, with the FCC media cross-ownership rule is changed at this juncture. FCC Chair Michael Powell stated that the market and competition will dictate the way media companies operate. The FCC promotes diversity, localism, and competition for the media industry. FCC actions in 2003 were said to be following the requirement for a biennial review of rules that was included in the 1996 Telecommunications Act. This means the issue will remain on the front burner. Media companies and their lobbyists will remain steadfast in their pursuit of the rule change. In turn, so will such opponents as the Prometheus Radio Project, which led the original federal lawsuit. The tension will remain as each side tries to put forth the best argument for changing or maintaining the status quo.

CONVERGENCE TRAINING

As the issue of cross-ownership winds its way through the FCC and courts, educators and others will continue, as a practical matter, to teach and train individuals for a converged environment. As discussed in chapter 1, the Seven Observations of Convergence are premised on creating best practices for media organizations in a converged world; the principles include communication, cooperation, and collaboration. The salience of these efforts lies in education and training as part of an organization's culture.

On the university level, chapter 7 discussed several schools that have started convergence curriculum or incorporated the use of technology in their courses, thereby ensuring the preparation of future journalists for converged working environments. How extensive or directed that education is depends on the mission and commitment of the university. Arguably, most academics would support the continued exposure to new technologies and their influence on media. The depth of a program's reach into convergence will advance as the professional world exhibits a need for such education. At this time, media managers are not identifying the need for *super journalists* who are capable of being all things to all platforms. However, there is support for educated and trained young journalists who can write and understand news values and who have an awareness and appreciation for a multimedia environment.

In print and broadcast newsrooms, the discussion varies among journalists on the role of convergence. Some find the movement to converged practices a natural progression, with new technologies increasing capabilities to gather and disseminate content. Some resent the implications that new skills and knowledge may be expected without training or compensation. As discussed earlier in this book, media managers have not created additional compensation venues for people who have expanded their skills in convergence. Performance reviews and some merit issues may tap into this area. Media executives must understand that their organizational culture is undergoing a seismic shift. The newsrooms of old are replaced with multimedia desks, cameras, digitization of content, and a more technologically savvy and proactive audience. It will not be beneficial to stand in place and refuse to make adjustments to content that is distributed. Nor will it be prudent to ignore the professionals needed to accomplish the goals of media organizations as they continue their use of newer technologies in a changing media market. These professionals must be compensated for their skills and expertise; therefore, managers must consider ways to include additional compensation as one of the best practices for a convergence model.

TELEPHONE/CABLE/INTERNET

It appears we may be in an era of information and content providers instead of media, telecommunications, Internet, and cable companies. Not only are the lines blending, but conglomeration of different industries is occurring. In chapter 7, we examined the pronouncement by SBC CEO Edward Whitacre (cited in Latour,

2004) that he wanted the telephone company to get into the TV business. Of course this is in response to digital delivery and the aging telephone industries being challenged by wireless, satellite, and cable modems. On the surface, Whitacre may be viewed as a corporate idealist with little support for such a venture. If we heed what happened with the convergence of AOL and Time Warner or AT&T and TCI cable, it would suggest that the merger of disparate businesses for content delivery cannot be successful. Yet the future holds potential for numerous arrangements that were unheard of in the past. Time Warner is considering acquiring Sprint wireless, which expands the content provider in another direction. This is an example of potential convergence that can occur not just across platforms, but industries as well, and change the delivery of information and entertainment content.

Fiberoptic cable increases the speed of delivery of data and can open new territory for a telephone company such as SBC. If SBC could offer audio, video, cable, and wireless in a package, an interested public might be listening. Currently, most people obtain these services from separate providers, but who would oppose one stop at an economical price? When the push to sign up users for broadband started in the early 2000s, critics suggested it would move slowly as people pondered adding another utility cost. In most instances, with LAN lines and broadband in the workplace, people made their connections when they arrived at work. Most media organizations acknowledge that the majority of their online traffic occurs from 9 a.m. to 5 p.m.—during the day when workers have access to employers' Internet connections. The convenience and accessibility of the home suggest there may be a market for a SBC telephone and TV company. The proof will be in the success of laying cable and making undisrupted connections at a reasonable price.

NEW TECHNOLOGIES

There are new technologies on the horizon that we have not yet considered. Historically, the adoption rate of new technologies was aligned with Paul Saffo's 30-year rule for new technologies to assimilate into society (cited in Fidler, 1997). However, the development cycle is much faster now as new and updated technologies appear simultaneously. For example, the cell phone capabilities have moved exponentially from analog to digital, providing voice mail, e-mail, text messaging, and video gaming options. As some people settled into buying cell phones for necessity as much as accessory, photo phones arrived and presented another dimension.

New hand-held devices such as individual DVD players, hand-held video game machines, Blackberrys, and PDAs offer ways to access content anywhere at any time. Media organizations, electronic manufacturers, and PC makers see a potential to include all kinds of content on these devices. People may want to communicate, but content providers want to increase the amount and type of content. It is not just talk. Want the latest sports scores? Stock reports? Breaking news? This is information that has a value, and newer devices are channels through which to sell this content.

We should watch for signs of more partnership and alliances across industries. As of this writing, SBC has a deal with EchoStar for satellite delivery of content, and Comcast, the number one cable company in the United States, seeks to offer voiceover Internet phone service (VOIP). The potential for such arrangements is enhanced by a convergence environment that supports more than one channel of delivery.

PRIVACY AND COPYRIGHT

The fascination with technology is understandable from the perspective of potential for news channels of communication. It is not just computers and the Internet, but wireless and satellite delivery that enhance connections. These new modes of delivery also present a cautionary tale for privacy and copyright concerns. Traditional media gatekeepers are no longer the only source for news, information, and entertainment. New portals and venues occur daily. What happens when everyone has open access to so much information and data? How will we continue to protect privacy and copyright concerns? The laws have not necessarily caught up with the technology. In 2002, the World Intellectual Property Organization (WIPO) issued a report that surveyed some of the issues on intellectual property and the Internet. Key issues identified were copyright protection in an electronic environment, liability for Internet service providers, linking copyright information online, peer-to-peer file sharing, and digital rights of broadcasters ("World Intellectual Property," 2002). Even from a global perspective, there are variations in what types of content are protected, and there is no uniformity across countries on enforcement.

From the media industry's perspective, companies try to manage the flow of information through electronic sources. By 2001, several online newspaper sites were requiring registration to access their sites past the homepage. This allows the company to (a) gather data about users through registration, and (b) be more aware of when people are accessing the sites. From an economic perspective, there are benefits to archival information, and most media outlets charge for this content after a certain period of time. The problem for traditional newspaper and broadcast outlets is that making their online sites unaccessible could be problematic in the long run. If the brand and reputation are to hold in the market, the public needs to be able to use the product. The nature of the Internet has been the spirit of open and free access. *The Wall Street Journal*, as discussed earlier, remains the premiere example of a successful subscription-only site. Although it has a specific targeted audience that it identified and reached, *The Journal* allowed the public free access to its online site for one week in November 2004. This was a strategic marketing ploy to expose more people to the product and experience growth. *The Journal* has thrived with a paid-subscription product online, and other media outlets are in pursuit of similar strategies for convergence operations. By 2003 there were at least 21 newspapers charging to access most content online (Sullivan, 2003). In 2005 the number increased to more than 35 newspapers charging access online ("Newspapers that change," 2005).

Marc Andreessen and Eric Bina were the creators of the Mosaic browser, which significantly impacted the Internet with its graphic interface. Andreessen once stated that one lesson learned from innovation was that, when discovering a new product, you cannot market it as *free* if you want people to pay (cited in Levy, 2003).

Andreessen's development of the graphic browser in the mid-1990s transformed the www portion of the Internet. This occurred largely at no cost to Internet users. Tribune Publishing President Jack Fuller expressed similar sentiments at the 2003 Online News Association conference in Chicago. Fuller stated the future of online journalism will include paid content. "We got everybody used to the idea that things that cost a lot of money to make ought to be available for absolutely nothing.... I think everyone will move, at least in part, to a model paid by the reader" (cited in O'Brien, 2003, pars. 2–3). Fuller contended that media will have to adapt to thrive in an online environment, and "journalists are experimenting our way to the future" (cited in O'Brien, 2003, par. 9). Fuller also said that online media have presented new opportunities and lessons for what a changing demographic, particularly young people, want from media. Media organizations want to make money from their Internet operations, but are challenged with how. There are incremental gains with archival data and advertisements. However, the jury is still out on such online advertisements as banner ads, pop-up ads, and subliminal ads, which are disturbing to online users. The push toward premium content on sites including Belo's dallascowboysplus.com or Tribune's bearstoday.com will be worth watching. These examples of sports premium sites are an attempt to capitalize on content and indicate that audiences may be willing to pay additional costs.

SUMMARY

I conclude that convergence is integral to the future of the media industry. As we rebound from the dotcom bust of 2001, more companies are expanding and experimenting with new approaches to content. By the publication of this book, the media organizations discussed will have morphed into another stage of convergence; what that will be varies for each media outlet. The research in this book—from in-depth interviews, participant observations, and internal and external documents—sheds light on convergence as a concept and process as it is currently operationalized in those organizations. Of course organizations continue to seek that "killer application," which will address a host of needs and objectives. This could be new hardware or software applications, but it is not a one-shot deal. The online operations of companies provide interactivity, audio, and video to complement offline operations. Wireless communication and new hand-held devices will provide new opportunities. What the public will adopt as the preferred mode of communication is the confounding variable with which every media, communication, and telecommunications organization must grabble—the unknown of human interest and need.

Technological innovations and their byproducts of new devices are tools that contribute to and enhance our ability to communicate and exchange information. I predict that media organizations will continue to embrace convergence or increase multimedia presentations for content adapted to their specific markets. The super journalist or super converged media organization is not the point. The goal should be creating accessibility and usability for the audience of media content and products. Each organization must pursue the best method to accomplish this goal. The Seven Observations of Convergence as best practices discussed in chapter 1 are a catalyst for moving in the right direction with a convergence business model. Each convergence operation will be customized to a particular market and its needs. Whatever the market or need, media content—information, news, or entertainment—should be readily accessible to all and have added value for the audience. As this chapter closes, a new one opens for convergence.

REFERENCES

Bear Stearns. (2003, June 2). *28-year newspaper-broadcast cross-ownership ban is over.* New York: Author.

Boczkowski, P. J. (2004). The processes of adopting multimedia and interactivity in three online newsrooms. *Journal of Communication, 54,* 197–213.

Damewood, A. (2004). New York Times publisher shares his vision for the future of journalism. Medill News [Electronic Version]. Retrieved March 8, 2004, from http://www.medill.northwestern.edu/insided/2004/sulzberger

FCC initiates proceedings to review newspaper broadcast cross-ownership. (2001, September 13). FCC News. Retrieved November 30, 2004, from http://ftp.fcc.gov/Bureaus/Mass_Media/News_Releases/2001/nrmm0109.html

Fidler, R. (1997). *Mediamorphosis: Understanding new media*. Thousand Oaks, CA: Pine Forge Press.

Hewitt, D. (2001). *Tell me a story*. New York: PublicAffairs™.

Latour, A. (2004, November 23). Meet the new TV guy: SBC's Whitacre revs up for video as cable, internet, eat into his phone business. *The Wall Street Journal*, pp. B1, B5.

Lenger, J. (2004, April 16). Happy 300th, American newspapers. *Editor & Publisher* [Electronic Version]. Retrieved April 16, 2004, from http://www.mediainfo.com/eandp/columns/shoptalkdisplay.jsp?vnu_content?id=1000490339

Levy, S. (2003, April 21). Out of left field: Andreessen did Mosaic, then Netscape. He was at the center of the browser wars and dot-com mania. What's he learned? *Enterprise, Newsweek, 151*(16), E10.

Newspaper Association of America. (2003). *Trends & numbers. Newspaper Association of America* [Electronic Version]. Retrieved June 1, 2003, from http://www.naa.org/artpage.cfm?AID=1610&SID=1022

Newspapers that change for their sites. (2005). Cyber Journalist. The Media Center at the American Press Institute. Retrieved January 18, 2005, from http://www.cyberjournalist.net/news/001818.php

O'Brien, K. (2003, November 14). Tribune's fuller: Future is paid content. Retrieved January 26, 2004, from http://www.journalists.org/2003conference/news/000036.html

Small papers can gain from media convergence. (2004, September 16). *The Casper Star-Tribune*. Retrieved September 23, 2004, from http://www.casperstartribune.net/articles/2004/09/16/news/regional/96f4be964aela41787256f1200

Sullivan, C. (2003, January 20). Information may want to be free, but even freedom has its limits. *Editor & Publisher, 136*(3), 22.

World Intellectual Property Organization. (2002). *Intellectual property on the internet: A survey of issues*. [Electronic Version]. Retrieved January 31, 2003, from http://ecommerce.wipo.int

Author Index

A

Aiman-Smith, L., 15
Albiniak, P., 38

B

Bagdikian, B. H., 30, 34
Bagozzi, R. P., 55
Ball-Rokeach, S. J., 8, 164, 178
Barringer, F., 6
Bernhardt, S. A., 163
Birge, E., 171–172
Blumler, J. G., 57
Boczkowski, P. J., 166, 177, 186
Bordia, P., 163
Bowman, S., 10
Brenner, D. L., 35
Brooks, B., 3
Budde, N., 50

C

Campbell, M., 53
Campbell, R., 10
Carey, J., 14, 60–62
Carlson, D., 43
Carlton, C., 132, 134
Carr, F., 12, 111–113
Castaneda, L., 172
Chandler, D., 161, 175
Compaine, B. M., 22, 28, 35
Conrad, K., 30
Criado, C. A. 171

D

Dasbach, A., 12, 21

Damewood, A., 183
David, P., 11
Davis, F. D., 55
De Sola Pool, I., 4
Dizard, W., 22, 43
Donnelly, J., 172
Dunham, P. J. 163
Dupagne, M. 55

E

Edler, J., 55–56
Eighmey, J., 58

F

Fidler, R., 53–55, 59, 196
Finberg, H., 151
Fine, J., 12
Fowler, M. S., 35
Frambach, R. T., 55–56
Fredin, E. S., 11

G

Gates, D., 13, 51
Gentry, J., 7
Gershon, R. A., 6
Goldhaber, G. M., 55
Gomery, D., 20, 27–28
Gonyea, D., 47
Gordon, R., 4, 102
Greenspan, R, 14
Griffith, T. I., 15
Gunkel, D. J., 176–177, 179
Gurevitch, M., 57

H

Haas, T., 70, 98, 128
Haiman, R. J., 9
Hancock, J. T., 163
Harrison, C. 168
Hewitt, D. 184
Higgins, J. M., 28
Hollifield, C. A., 56
Horan, L., 170
Hoyt, M., 47

I, J

Iosifides, P., 33
Jenkins, H., 162–165

K

Kampinsky, E., 10
Katz, E., 57
Kawamato, K., 43
Kelley, C., 4, 9
Kennedy, G., 3
Kiesler, S., 164
Killebrew, K. C., 162
Kolodzy, J., 31
Kraeplin, C. 171
Kramer, R. 163
Kraut, R., 164

L

Latour, A., 168–169, 194
Lenger, J., 189
Levy, S., 197
Lin, C. A., 55
Lin, S., 58
Lindemann, C., 87
Lipinski, A. M., 70
Lundmark, V., 164

M

Magretta, J., 19
Matei, S., 164, 178
Mattheson, D., 165
McChesney, R. W., 30, 34
McCord, L., 58
McLuhan, M., 9

McManus, J., 34–35
McQuail, D., 57
Meyer-Krahmer, F., 55–56
Mintz, J., 165
Moen, D. R., 3
Moses, L., 51, 87
Mukopadhyay, T., 164
Munk, N., 21, 29
Murphy, J., 127

N

Napoli, P., 31–33
Negroponte, N., 4, 7–8, 177

O

O'Brien, K., 198
O'Keefe, G. J., 58
Ozanich, G. W., 28–29

P

Patterson, M., 164
Pavlik, J. V., 38
Postmes, T. 164
Powell, M. K., 173–174

R

Ranly, D., 3
Rayburn, J. D., 57
Reichert, T., 157, 166
Rogers, E. M., 19, 43–45, 55–57,
    62, 98
Ruggiero, T. E., 19, 56–57

S

Saba, J., 28
Sakasena, S., 56
Schaffer, J., 5
Scherlis, W., 164
Seib, P., 3
Silverthorne, S., 56
Smythe, D., 15
Standage, T., 57
Steinbock, D., 12–13, 50
Sudhoff, D., 172

Sulanowski, B. K. 58
Sullivan, C., 52, 197
Surowiecki, J., 10

T

Tanis, M., 164
Taylor, C. P., 163
Thelen, G., 57, 99
Tidd, J., 56
Toffler, A., 177
Tompkins, A., 22

V

Vishwanath, A., 55

W

Walther, J. B., 164
Warshaw, P. R., 55
Webster, J. G., 58
Wendland, M., 7, 21
Westbrook, B., 168
Willis, C., 10
Wirth, M. O., 28–29
Wirtz, B. W., 3

Y

Yerton, S., 167

Z

Zammuto, R. F., 15
Zavoina, S., 157, 166

Subject Index

A

ABC, 37, *see also*
  Big Three networks
All the news that's fit to print
  slogan, 49
Amazon.com, 10
American Press Institute (API), 3, 7,
  175, 188
  americanpressinstitute.com, 7
  see Convergence Tracker, 7, 175,
    188–189
  Media Center, 3, 60–61
AOL, 4, 8, 21, 29, 46, 48, 54, 168,
  195
AOL/Time Warner, 29, 35
Apple iPod, 167
AT&T, 169, 195
Arizona Republic, 12, *see also*
  convergence in Phoenix

B

Backpack journalist, 172
Ball State University, 170–171, 175
  Center for Media Design, 170
Bear Stearns, 192
Being Digital, 4, 7
Belo Corp., 7, 18, 20, 36, 39, 51,
  127, 129, 143, 145, 155,
  158, 184
  Annual report 2001–2003,
    155–157
  Belo Interactive Dallas, 9,
    127–131, 134–136, 140,
    142, 149, 151, 155–156
  Cowboysplus.com, 132

Dallas Morning News, The, 20,
  51, 127–128, 130, 132,
  134, 140, 142–146, 149,
  155–156
Dallasnews.com, 21, 128, 130,
  132, 140, 151, 154–155
Dallas Web Sites Mission, 135,
  137
Dallas Web Sites Style and Oper-
  ation Guide, 135
GuideLive.com, 130, 151,
  153–154
Market dominance, 127–128
moat speech, 144
Quick, 134
TXCN cable, 20, 127–130, 132,
  140, 142, 144–146
WFAA-TV, 20, 127–130, 132,
  140–146, 149, 151, 155
BIGresearch of Ohio, 61
Big Three networks, 37
  see also ABC; CBS; NBC
Boston News-Letter, The, 189
Brand, 103, 187, 197
Broadband, 88, 183,195
Broadcast license renewal, 36
BSkyB, 38
Business model, 14,
  convergence, 188
  registration, subscription, adver-
    tising, 14, 52
  fee or percentage, 48
  sign-up or subscription, 48
  paid/fee hybrid, 52
  premium paid, 132
  multimedia content sharing and
    cross-promotion, 74

C

Capital Cities/ABC, 28
Case studies of convergence pioneers,
    4, 187, *see also*
    Tribune Company, 69
    Media General, 97
    Belo Corp., 127
CBS, 37, 184, *see also* Big Three
    networks
Center for Digital Democracy, 20, 38
CitySearch, 152
Civil Rights Forum on Communica-
    tions Policy, 38
Cleveland Plain Dealer, The, 51
Cleveland.com, 52
    WXYC-TV, 52
    PAX-TV, 52
    Sun Newspapers, 52
Columbia Journalism Review, 73,
    98, 129
    Who Owns What, 73, 98
Comcast cable, 29, 169, 196
Constitution, U.S., 30, 36
Communications Act of 1934,
    36–37
Conglomeration, 30, *see also* merg-
    ers and acquisitions
Content, 4
    computer-driven, 56
    deliver, 4, 54
    digitization, 7
    providers, 8, 16, 48
    repurposing, 145–146
Content management systems, 52,
    105, 185
    Oxygen, 53, 185
    BudgetBank, 53, 105,107, 109,
        123, 185
    Nando Media, 53
Convergence in Phoenix, 12
    see also Arizona Republic
    KPNX-TV
Convergence, many faces of, 3
    audience perspective, 43
    concept and process, 6, 19, 23,
        78, 111, 157, 166, 184,
        187, 198
    definitions, 3–4
    economic benefits, 147
    journalistic perspective, 3

marketing and promoting, 118
    multimedia applications, 3
    organizational perspective, 43, 81
    window of opportunity, 6
Convergence definition model, 5
Convergence models, 12, *see also*b
    usiness model
Convergence pioneers, 186–187, *see
    also*
    Belo
    Media General
    Tribune Company
Convergence training, 193
Cross-platform training, 171
Cross-promotion of media, 69, 84,
        90, 119, 167, 180
Cultural convergence, 164

D

Dallas Herald, The, 128
Department of Commerce, U.S., 60
Department of Defense, U.S., 4
Designated market areas, (DMA), 192
Detnews.com, 47–48
Detroit News, The, 46–48, 187
Detroit Free Press, The, 46–47, 187
Detroit Newspaper Agency, The, 47
Detroit newspaper strike, 48
Diffusion of Innovations, 43
Diffusion of innovations theory, 19,
        40, 62, *see also* innovation
        process in an organization,
        five stages
Digital divide, 179
Digital spectrum giveaway, 176
Digital video recorder, (DVR), 186
Digitization of media and informa-
        tion technology, 6
DirecTV, 37–38
Disney, 29
Disney/ABC, 35
Disruptive technologies, 55–56
Diversity principle, 31
    source, 31–32
    content, 31–32
    exposure, 31–32
Dot.com bust of 2001, 51, 87, 90,
        119, 151, 198
Drudge Report, 17

E

E-book, 10–11
Echo Star's Dish Network, 38, 196
Economies of scale, 185
Emerging technologies, 8, 27, 33, 37, 44, 55–56, 112, 179, 184
Evening News Association, 46
Expedia, 130

F

Face to face communication, 164, 178
Fairness and Accuracy in Reporting, 38
Federal Communications Commission (FCC), 20, 31, 35–38, 169
  cross-ownership rule change 2003, 53, 72, 171, 191
  diversity, localism, competition, 31
Federal district court Philadelphia rejects rule change, 20, 38 53, 72, 191
Fiduciary responsibility, 29
First Amendment, 30, 36
Follow the money, axiom, 33
Fort-Worth Star Telegram, 150
Fourth estate, 27
Fox network, 37
Frank N. Magid Associates, 22
Functionality of a web site, 152–154

G

Gannett, 35, 46, 189–190, 193, *see also* convergence in Phoenix
Gannett News Department, 189
Gatekeeping, 18, 161
GE (General Electric), 29–30, *see also* NBC Universal
Gutenberg, 177, 185

H

High definition TV, (HDTV), 176
Horizontal integration, 30, *see also* mergers and acquisitions

Houston Chronicle, 166
Hughes Corp., 37
Hyper text markup language (HTML), 165

I

Incredibles, The, 167, 178
Information-driven society, 6
Innovation champion, 98
Innovation management, 55–56
Innovation process in an organization, five stages, 19, 44–45, 53, 55, 177
  agenda setting, 43–45
  matching, 43–45, 48
  redefining/restructuring, 43, 45, 51–52
  clarifying, 43, 45, 52–53
  routinizing, 43, 45, 53
Insider, The, 36
Interactive potential, 10
Internet portals, 46, *see also* AOL, Prodigy
Internet service provider (ISP), 48, 54

J

J-Lab, 190–191
Joint operating agreement, (JOA), 187
Journalism practices, 166

K

KPNX-TV, NBC affiliate, 12, *see also* convergence in Phoenix

L

Layering the news, 115
Life. Printed Daily, 102–103
Lilly Endowment, 170

M

Market Driven Journalism, 35

Marketplace approach, 35
Marketplace of ideas, 27, 30–31, 34
  economic-based theory, 31
  democratic-based theory, 31,
  diversity of ideas, 33,
  diversity of products, 33, *see*
    also diversity principle
McNeil Lehrer Hour, 100
Media Audit, The, 14
Media dependency theory, 8
Media effects, 19
Media General, 7, 12, 16, 18, 20–21,
    36, 39, 97–99, 105, 108,
    119, 122, 184
  annual reports 2001–2003,
    119–122
  News Center, The, 7, 12, 16, 97,
    100, 105, 111, 115,
    118–119, 121
  News Center Pledge, The, 112
  *News Channel 8 Statement of
    Philosophy, The*, 112,
    114
  Tampa Tribune, The, 12, 21, 57,
    97–98, 105, 108–109,
    112, 117–118
  Temple to convergence, 16, 97–98
  TBO.com, 12, 21, 97, 108,
    112–113, 115
  WFLA-TV, 11–12, 21, 97, 108,
    111–112, 116–118, 120
Media information palette, (MIP),
    165, 167, 177, 180
Media literacy, 33
Mediamorphosis, 53–55
  six fundamental principals, 54
MediaNews Group, 188
Media organizations, 5–6
  Platforms, 6
Mergers and acquisitions, 4, 28, 30,
    35
  three phases, 28–29
  see also conglomeration, hori-
    zontal integration, verti-
    cal integration
Microsoft, 16, 168
Microsoft Sidewalk, 152
Milwaukee Journal, 132
Mini case study, 46, *see also*
    Detnews.com
  Detroit News, The,
  Detroit Free Press, The

Detroit Newspaper Agency, The
  Detroit newspaper strike
Missouri Group, 3
MIT Media Lab, 162
Mosaic graphic browser, 6, 197
Multimedia, 3, 116, 121, 123
  applications, 3
  desk, 113, 194
  dimension, 173
  environment, 5, 19, 172
  journalism operations, 74
  liaison, 113
  newsroom, 99
  platforms, 118
  presentations, 199
  stories, 188
  storytelling, 191
Multimedia stories, 188
Multitasking, 163

N

Napster, 178
National Council of the Churches of
    Christ, 20
National Newspaper Association, 188
National Rifle Association, 20
National TV ownership cap, 36
*Nation Online, A: How Americans
    Are Expanding Their Use
    of the Internet*, 60
NBC, 37
  see also Big Three networks
New media, 10, 17
  research, 59
News Corp, 35, 37, 51
News Journal, The, 190
New Jersey Online, 166
Newspaper Association of America,
    12, 84
Newspaper/broadcast cross-owner-
    ship rule, FCC, 21, 36, 53,
    72, 128, 175, 186–187, 191
Newspaper readership penetration,
    22
New technologies, 195
New York Newsday, 73
New York Times Digital, 17
New York Times, The, 17, 36, 38,
    49, 166, 183
Niche audiences, 22
Nielsen Media Research, 6

Nielsen/NetRatings, 58

O

One-way model of communication,
     5, 8
Online advertising, 198
     pop-up ads, 198
     subliminal ads, 198
     banner ads, 198
Online Journalism Review, 172
Online News Association, 151
Online Publishers Association, 22
Online registration of web sites, 52
Organizational cultural change, 17,
     21, 82, 100, 105, 115, 117,
     185
Oxford English Dictionary, 4

P

Paid subscription model, 12, 13, 49,
     132, 197, *see also* business
     model
Peer-to-peer file sharing, 197
Pew Center for Civic Journalism, 5
Pittsburgh Post-Gazette, 132
Popular culture, 167
Portraits of Grief, 49
Poynter Institute, 9, 97
Priceline, 130
Principle of relative constancy, 180
Privacy and copyright, 196
Prodigy, 46, 48
Project for Excellence in Journalism,
     28
Promethus Radio Project, 20, 38, 193
Public affairs knowledge, 33
Public sphere, 174, 184
Pulitzer Prizes, 31, 92, 94
Push and pull technology, 8, 17

R

Readership.org, 130
Reagan/Bush administrations, 35
Recording Industry of America, the,
     178
Registration process, online news-
     papers, 18

Regulation, 34, 173
     deregulation, 35–36
     weaknesses, 38
Rules of engagement, 78

S

SBC, 194–196
SBC Yahoo, 168
Scopes Monkey Trial, 69
Scorecard, 109–110
Scrolling on the Internet, 10
Segmentation of audiences, 18
Seven Observations of Convergence,
     15, 18, 111, 132, 141, 148,
     193, 199
     see also communication, 15,
          111, 132, 141–142, 193
     commitment, 15, 111, 141, 143
     cooperation, 16, 111, 132, 193
     compensation, 16, 141, 148, 194
     cultural, 16, 141–142, 148, 150
     competition, 17, 148
     customer, 17, 111
Shovelware, 44, 54, 187
*Simultaneous Media Use Survey,
     The*, 60–61
60 Minutes, 36, 184
Social capital, 161
Sociocultural implications, 161–162,
     179–180
Social economic status (SES), 59
Social/organic convergence, 163
     social responsibility of media or-
          ganizations, 22
*Springfield (Missouri) News-Leader,
     The*, 190
Sprint, 195
State of the News Media, 2004, 28,
     51
     three economic models, 51
          subscription based
          registration
          mix of paid and free content
Stock merger, 4
Structured query language (SQL), 107
Synergistic behavior, 31, 37, 70

T

TCI Communications, 169, 195

Teaching convergence, 169–173
Technological determinism, 161,
        175–177,
    see also hard determinism, 177
    soft determinism, 177
    technological innovations, 179,
        183–184, 199
Technologies of Freedom, 4
Telecommunications Act, 1996, 20,
        31, 35–36, 38, 173, 193
Telphone/cable/internet, 194
Theoretical implications, 43
    failed technologies, 43
    see also diffusion of innovations
        theory
    uses and gratifications
    innovation management
30-year-rule, Paul Saffo's, 54, 59, 195
Time, 179
Time Warner, 4, 8, 21, 29, 35, 179,
        195
TiVo, 141
Traditional media and business
        practices, 27
Tribune Company, 7, 18, 20, 31, 36,
        38, 39, 52, 69–70, 72–73,
        78, 81, 83–84, 86, 90, 94,
        184–186, 193, 198
    annual reports, 2001–2003, 91–94
    Blackvoices.com, 75–76
    Chicago convergence themes and
        trends, 95
    ChicagoSports.com, 76
    Chicagotribune.com, 48, 76, 83
    Chicago Tribune, 20, 48, 69–70,
        72–74, 76, 80, 89
    CLTV cable, 20, 72–76, 80, 83,
        85, 88, 92
    Electronic News group, 78, 89
    Hartford Courant, 81
    Los Angeles Times, 31, 73, 92
    Metromix.com, 72, 75–76, 84–86,
        89
    Newsday, 92
    Orlando Sentinel, 21
    Times Mirror, 20, 31, 38
    Traditional convergence pioneer,
        70
    Tribune Content Sharing, 77–78
    Shared News Service, 78
    WGN-TV and radio, 20, 69–70,
        72, 77, 83, 85

WTIC-TV, 81
Tulsa World, The, 13
TulsaWorld.com, 13
Two-way communication, 6, 165

U

Ubiquitous nature of media, 11
Usability of a web site, 152
Uses and gratifications, 19, 40,
        56–59
U.S. Supreme Court, 40

V

Vertical integration, 30
    see also mergers and acquisi-
        tions
Viacom/CBS, 35
Victorian Internet, The, 57
Video display terminals, (VDT), 178,
        185
Videographers, 52, 116
Vinn circles, 8
Visual journalists (VJs), 21
Vivendi Universal, 29
Voice over internet phone service,
        (VOIP), 196

W

Wall Street Journal, The, 12–13,
        36, 49–50, 132, 197
    Dow Jones Co., 12, 50
    Wall Street Journal Interactive,
        50
    Wsj.com, 12, 49–50
    Wall Street Journal Radio Net-
        work, 50
*Web Habit, The: An Ethnographic
        Study of Web Usage*, 60–61
Wireless fidelity, (Wi-Fi), 179
World Greatest Newspaper (WGN),
        69
World Intellectual Property Organi-
        zation, (WIPO), 196
World Trade Center, 49

Y

Yahoo, 16–17